The Vivarium

by the same authors

*

THE BOOK OF THE GARDEN POND
(*Stanley Paul, 1958*)

FRESHWATER TROPICAL AQUARIUM FISHES
(*Spring Books, 1963*)

The Vivarium

GEORGE F. HERVEY
& JACK HEMS

ILLUSTRATED BY
EILEEN M. HILL

FABER AND FABER
24 Russell Square
London

First published in mcmlxvii
by Faber and Faber Limited
24 Russell Square London WC1
Printed in Great Britain by
Latimer Trend & Co Ltd Plymouth

© *George F. Hervey and Jack Hems 1967*

Contents

Illustrations

>>>

PLATES

9

Illustrations

FIGURES

Preface

⫸⫸⫸⫸⫸⫸⫸⫸⫸⫸⫸⫸⫸⫸⫸⫸⫸⫸⫸⫸⫸⫸⫸⫸⫸⫸⫸⫸⫸⫸⫸⫸⫸⫸⫸

It is hardly necessary for us to point out that this book is not an exhaustive one. The size precludes it. So far as we are aware no exhaustive work on vivaria has as yet been written, and we doubt it ever will. The reason is not far to seek. It is reliably estimated that some 5,000 species of lizards and snakes, 2,000 species of frogs and toads, 300 species of tortoises and terrapins and 200 species of newts and salamanders, are known to naturalists. Even if only a third of them are suitable to be kept in captivity, without the alligators and caymans, the gharial and crocodiles (though comparatively few), they would demand a work of several volumes, and a corps of specialists, to be given adequate treatment.

This book, therefore, aims at nothing higher than to present the reader with the general principles of vivaria, and some information about a few amphibians and reptiles that are suited to live in them. It is, in fact, designed for he who, as an alternative to the lily pool and the ubiquitous goldfish in his garden, might prefer a small enclosure for frogs and toads; and for he who, as an alternative to the tropical aquarium in his house, might prefer a case of lizards or non-venomous snakes.

In order to avoid confusion we have used the scientific names of the species along with their popular names, but we have made no attempt to check them with the most recent

11

Preface

system of nomenclature, still more to arrange our work in accordance with scientific classification. It is not due to laziness or ignorance on our part, but to the fact that this book has not been designed as a work of reference but as a general work to be read, and we hope enjoyed, by all who are interested in the keeping of amphibians and reptiles as pets. For the same reason we have refrained from footnotes, cross references, references to sources, and bibliographies. Our one concession to pedantry is the inclusion of a short index to help the reader to find his way about.

For the rest, we have to thank Miss Eileen M. Hill, who has illustrated our previous books, for once again coming to our help with her life-like pen. That this book is not so copiously illustrated as our others is no fault of hers. It is due entirely to the fact that as, apart from markings and size which are mentioned in the text, one frog is much like another, one newt much like another, and so on, and everyone knows what frogs and newts, tortoises and snakes, look like; to illustrate more than a few members of each group would be over-much.

GEORGE F. HERVEY & JACK HEMS

1

The Vivarium and its Inhabitants

>>>

The word vivarium (plural vivaria) derives from the Latin
vivus = living, and in its widest sense denotes an artificially prepared place in which land animals (as opposed to
aquatic animals which are kept in aquaria) are kept alive in as
nearly as possible their natural state. Strictly, therefore, a
zoological garden is a vivarium. Once it was so and in a map
of Great Britain, drawn about the year 1250, Windsor Forest
is marked 'vivarium'. Nowadays, however, the word is
rarely used in such a wide sense; it is more usually restricted
to mean an enclosure in which small amphibians and reptiles
are kept.

At its best a vivarium is easily made. In a part of the garden
that is neither in full sun nor in total shade (because though
amphibians and reptiles seek the shade, some sunlight is
essential for their health) sink a pond and stock it with
plants to keep the water clear. Alongside it build a low
rockery, with ferns for shade, alpine plants for colour and
beauty, and rocks and stones for hiding places. Finally, sur-
round the whole with a three-foot wall (stone is more pleasing
than brick) with an inwards over-hanging edge to prevent
escapes (Fig. 1). No more is necessary, but if the enclosure
is a small one, protection from birds and cats may be given
to the inmates by covering it with wire netting.

Ideally the pond should be made by digging an irregular

saucer-shaped depression, ramming the earth firm, and lining it with concrete, which must then be seasoned by scouring it several times in changes of water. Since only a small pond is necessary, no elaborate preparation is required. A satisfactory mix is one part of cement, two of washed sand and three of ballast (all measured in a bucket) and mixed in a dry condition. Mixing must be continued until the agglomeration is of a uniform colour, free from streaks of brown and grey. A small quantity of water is then added, and the mixing

Fig. 1. Outdoor Vivarium

continued (more water being added from time to time) until the shovel plunged into the mixture and withdrawn with a few jerks, leaves small ridges that retain their formation. The work should be done on a wooden platform with a clean shovel; for if earth enters the mixture a crack will develop in the finished work.

The concrete should be laid as soon as possible after mixing and all in one day. It should be spread evenly over the excavation and rammed down in order to remove any air pockets.

The Vivarium and its Inhabitants

Rain setting in after concrete has been laid does no harm. Indeed, within reason, the longer concrete takes to dry the harder it sets, so that, as soon as the concrete has been laid, damp sacks should be thrown over it to retard drying, and in hot weather they may have to be moistened daily.

After the sacking has been removed, the concrete should be given a rendering coat consisting of one part of cement and three parts of sand mixed with water to the consistency of thick cream, and laid on smoothly with a trowel to a thickness of about half an inch. It should be kept moist with damp sacking for about three or four days.

In our opinion a concrete pond is always the most satisfactory and cannot be bettered. However, it involves a good deal of hard work. It is, therefore, less laborious, but more expensive to buy a pond readymade of fibre glass. At worst, a pond can be made by sinking into the ground a watertight half-barrel or large kitchen sink, the plug hole filled with cement. The top edge may be hidden with rocks and plants.

One part of the pond should be at least fifteen inches deep, to protect against frost those creatures that hibernate at the bottom of the water. The pond should be filled with two or three inches of loam, covered with an inch or two of well-washed coarse sand or grit.

Suitable plants for stocking such a pond are water starwort (*Callitriche*), Canadian water weed (*Elodea*), water milfoil (*Myriophyllum*), water violet (*Hottonia*) and water crowfoot (*Ranunculus*). All are perennial and grow submerged, but expose their flowers above the surface so that there is ample colour without need to plant a water lily or spatterdock. They are easy to plant. With a notched stick in each hand, the stem or roots of the plant are pressed no more than an inch into the sand with one stick, and held there while the sand is raked back with the other.

For a rock garden good drainage is essential. The ground should be dug out to a depth of about two feet and the hole layered to a depth of about nine or ten inches with clinkers, unsifted ashes or broken bricks. Over this should be spread a layer of old turves, grass-side down. The soil that was thrown up when the drainage course was dug should be piled up with a liberal mixture of sand and grit, and stones of all sizes broken up in it. The stones should be set tilting slightly backwards, so that the rain runs into the earth, and it gives a better and more natural effect to have a few large stones just jutting above the surface of the ground than many small ones dotted here and there like almonds on a cake. The rockery should not be too high: a couple of feet is ample, and the surrounding wall should be sufficiently distant to prevent an escape by a jump from the top of the rockery to the top of the wall.

Planting the rock garden calls for no special skill, and a wide range of plants is available. For covering a bare patch in record time we strongly recommend snow in summer (*Cerastium*). As the name implies, the rockfoils or saxifrages, such as London pride, are excellent plants for growing in rockeries, as also are the stonecrops or sedums, particularly *Sedum spectabile* from Japan, which attracts butterflies, and the houseleeks or sempervivums.

Many other plants are available, but those that we have suggested are perennial. They come up every year and grow rampantly, thereby reducing the work of maintenance to little more than keeping the vivarium tidy by thinning out surplus plants and removing dead leaves and other débris.

In fact a colony of frogs, toads and newts, living under the conditions we have outlined will be largely self-supporting. Natural food, in the form of insects, will be attracted by the plants in the rockery, and more can be attracted by laying down pieces of raw meat. Occasionally some earthworms, wood lice, caterpillars and other small creatures from the garden may be thrown over the wall, but not between October and April which is the hibernating period. Care should always be taken to avoid food falling into the pond. A small body of water is very quickly polluted by uneaten food, and, when it is, the water has to be changed at once. This is a nuisance; for as it is hardly worth the trouble of making an outlet for a small pond, the water either has to be siphoned or bailed out, with the precaution of seeing that no small animals are siphoned or bailed out with it.

A vivarium built on these lines is the best way of keeping our native amphibians and the hardy species from abroad. It is also suitable for hardy snakes, provided they are kept by themselves. They must not, of course, be kept with amphibians because they are carnivorous and in the wild feed on frogs and similar creatures. Tortoises may also be kept in the outdoor vivarium, but as they are vegetarian, and very greedy feeders, they do considerable damage to the plants. In our experience, however, they will not touch thrift, creeping jenny, erica or heathers, and dwarf conifers, which, therefore, may be planted instead. Certainly the vivarium is the best place in which to keep tortoises. If they are given the freedom of the garden, at best they will do considerable damage to the plants, and at worst they will wander away. They may, of course, be confined in a wire run or a large lidless and bottomless box of sufficient height to prevent them putting their front legs on the top edge and hoisting themselves out, but neither looks attractive in a well-kept garden.

An indoor vivarium may take many forms. A readymade vivarium is sold in pet shops. It is little more than a wooden box with a sloping glass roof, a small service door at the back, and a tray (as in a birdcage) to facilitate cleaning. It has the merit of convenience and is easy to keep clean, but it is not an attractive ornament for a room, and is usually much too small. A vivarium should never be less than twenty-four inches long, and three feet is considerably better.

A very satisfactory and ornamental vivarium can be made out of a large glass tank (as sold in pet shops for keeping fish) with a close-fitting cover of wire gauze, so that the inmates can breathe but not escape (Fig. 2). The furnishings will depend on the animals that are to be housed in it.

B   17

The Vivarium and its Inhabitants

For snakes and lizards it is enough to cover the bottom with an inch or two of dry sand, over which may be spread some dry spaghnum moss or pine needles. Skinks and animals that burrow, however, will need a deeper layer of sand. Small branches of trees and rocks will give a decorative effect, and supply the inmates with suitable hiding places. A shallow bowl of drinking water should be sunk to its rim in the sand. If it is necessary to keep the vivarium heated, the handyman will know of many ways. The best is with a thermostatically-controlled electrical element, of the type designed for use in the miniature greenhouse in which amateur horticulturists grow cacti and succulents.

Toads and salamanders favour a well-aerated floor covered with damp garden soil mixed with peat, and a layer of damp moss. Rocks and logs of wood furnish decoration and provide hiding places, and, of course, provision must be made to supply enough drinking water. The soil should be clean, not that which has been fouled by domestic pets, and if peat is not available a good substitute is sawdust that has been allowed to stand outdoors in wind and rain for several weeks. Aeration may be provided by layering the bottom of the vivarium with small stones (each about the size of a pea) and over it a layer of rather larger stones or granite chippings.

For frogs, newts and small terrapins, a different form of furnishing is necessary, because they must have water in which to swim. The tank should be layered with an inch of sand and filled with water to a depth of about five or six inches. Rockwork should be built up until it stands out of the water, and be so arranged that the animals can crawl easily on to it. Moss should be provided for them to hide in. If heat is necessary, we recommend a thermostatically-controlled electrical immersion heater, of the type sold in pet shops for tropical aquaria. In order to keep the water clear, some bog or marsh plants, such as water purslane (*Ludwigia palustris*) and brooklime (*Veronica beccabunga*) for the unheated vivarium, and hair grass (*Eleocharis*) and bacopa

18

The Vivarium and its Inhabitants

(*Herpestis*) for the heated vivarium, should be planted in the
sand. Suitable submerged plants, as recommended for aquaria,
may also be planted. A vivarium furnished on these lines is
sometimes called an aqua-vivarium (Fig. 2). It should be kept

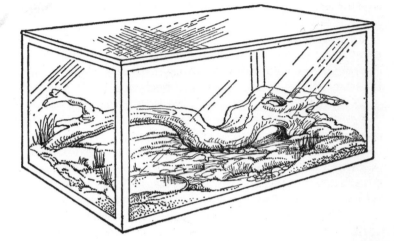

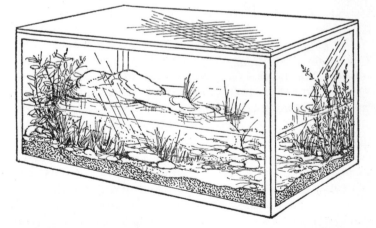

Fig. 2. Indoor Vivarium (above); Aqua-Vivarium (below)

covered with a close-fitting cover of wire-gauze (as recommended for vivaria) or with a sheet of glass (as recommended for aquaria) if it is to be heated. Provision should be made to facilitate cleaning. Most of the creatures that are kept in aqua-vivaria make plenty of excreta; terrapins would be swimming in their own urine if they were left too long without a change of water.

An indoor vivarium needs light, and plenty of it if it is planted. At the same time, care should be taken not to situate it where the sun will fall directly on it for any length of time. It is best, therefore, to shade the back and sides, either by painting them or by covering them with paper, and to stand the vivarium about two or three feet from a window that faces north, east or west, in that order, and never south.

Every habitation, from a royal palace to a dog-hole, has to be cared for and kept clean. A vivarium is no exception, but has the advantage that it is more or less trouble free and needs far less attention than most animal habitations.

For all practical purposes an outdoor vivarium looks after itself. The gardener may find some work to do among the rockery and plants, but otherwise there is little to be done other than to supply fresh drinking water daily and change the water in the pond if it becomes foul.

The indoor vivarium needs rather more attention; for as well as fresh drinking water daily and a change of bathing water when necessary, periodically the fouled sand, the withered branches of trees and other furnishings have to be removed and replaced by fresh.

The keynote is to keep the vivarium, whether outdoor or indoor, as clean as possible, and common sense dictates what chores are necessary to this end. Overcrowding must be avoided at all costs; for, as among human beings, overcrowding breeds slum conditions and invites disease.

With regular cleaning, however, no overcrowding, and fresh food and water, disease among animals kept in vivaria is rare. It is as well, because little is known about the diseases that attack amphibians and reptiles and the parasites that infest them. Inevitably so, of course, because medical science must first be directed towards human ailments and then towards those of farm and domestic animals. Until more is known of these things, a study of the diseases of the lower animals can never be more than the pastime of the biologist.

As a result, satisfactory drugs for the internal complaints of amphibians and reptiles are more or less unknown. Santonin is recommended for intestinal worms in tortoises and terrapins. For a large tortoise (five pounds or over) one grain should be powdered and sprinkled on its food; for a large terrapin a quarter of a grain is recommended. At least two doses at ten-day intervals will be necessary. For smaller animals the dose should be proportionately less. No other internal drugs are to be recommended, though raw garlic is said to be a good vermifuge for those reptiles that will take it.

All other treatments are external, dictated largely by common sense. Thus shell erosion, caused by a deficiency of calcium or, in the case of terrapins, by having been kept in very dirty or acid water, should be combated by frequent changes of water which, if acid, may be improved by the addition of a teaspoonful of powdered chalk, egg-shell or cuttlefish bone to every gallon of water. The food should be sprinkled with chalk or cuttlefish, or lightly smeared with cod-liver or halibut-liver oil. Treatment should be coupled with giving the animal as much direct sunlight as possible, and the affected parts of the shell should be cleaned by painting with iodine (care being taken to avoid it coming into contact with the soft parts of the body) repeated every second or third day. In extreme cases the eroded area may be filled with equal parts of plaster of Paris and oxide of zinc, mixed to a paste with a little water.

Common sense, too, dictates that eyes that have become encrusted after winter hibernation should be bathed with a mild solution of boracic crystals, or smeared with a little golden eye ointment; and that cuts and sores on the body should be dressed with a watered down solution of peroxide of hydrogen or with penicillin ointment.

Reptiles, no less than human beings, are subject to pneumonia, and the symptoms are much the same: lethargy, loss of appetite, dulled eyes, a running nose, and, in tortoises, a discharge from the mouth. Little can be done except to give extra warmth (at least ten degrees Fahrenheit above normal) with adequate ventilation but complete protection from cold air. Tempting foods, with a little cod-liver or halibut-liver oil, are helpful, and cases taken in hand early have been known to respond to inhalations of friar's balsam. A teaspoonful of balsam to a pint of boiling water is placed in a bowl in the vivarium, which should be covered with a sheet of glass or a board to retain the steam.

It is the rule, rather than the exception, for newly-imported reptiles to be infested with crab-like, blood-sucking insects, commonly called ticks. The reptile should be taken in hand, and the ticks removed with a forceps after first touching them with a drop of paraffin oil or methylated spirit to cause them to loosen their hold. During the operation, as at all times when necessary, a snake should be held firmly but not tightly just behind the head. The closer to the head that a snake is held the less opportunity it has of biting.

Periodically snakes cast their outer skin. It occurs at irregular intervals; perhaps every fortnight, perhaps every three or four months. Snakes about to slough invariably refuse food and for some days before the event the scales covering the eyes are seen to be cloudy or whitish. The snake may now spend a good deal of time in the water, for this helps in the detachment of the skin. Soon the skin splits about the lips, and the snake peels it off from the head downwards by rubbing its body against rough surfaces. If the sloughing is incomplete it is as well to help the snake by peeling it off with the hands; if this is not done, septic sores are likely to form between the old and new skins.

The Vivarium and its Inhabitants

Diseases among amphibians present us with greater problems than among reptiles, because the regular germicides invariably do more harm than good. Iodine and potash permanganate are said to be fatal to newts, if not to all amphibians, as is carbolic acid in any form, and to reptiles as well.

Among newts and salamanders virtually nothing is known about a disease (commonly called newt pest) that manifests itself as bloody patches and raised swellings on the body. All that can be done is to isolate those specimens that have been attacked and keep them in a clean container with frequent changes of water. The vivarium from which they have been taken should be thoroughly cleansed and re-furnished with fresh sand and other material.

Frogs and toads that have been kept in a dirty vivarium, or in an overcrowded one, are sometimes attacked by a disease that shows itself as a cheesy substance partly embedded in the skin. The affected areas should be swabbed with four teaspoonfuls of boracic crystals dissolved in a pint of water, repeated as often as may be necessary and the areas then dressed with friar's balsam.

Fungus diseases that appear on the skin are best treated by wiping the affected animals very gently with a soft rag dipped in paraffin, rinsing them in clean water, and placing them in a vivarium with plenty of mud on the bottom.

The toes of amphibians, if badly affected with gangrene, may be amputated with a sharp, clean razor blade and dressed with friar's balsam. The operation is a painless one.

The frogs, toads, newts and salamanders belong to the Class Amphibia, from the two Greek words *amphi* = on both sides, and *bios* = life; a name given to them because they live both in water and on land.

Amphibians inhabit the damper places, or else have become secondarily adapted to a completely aquatic life, but always in fresh water because no amphibian can tolerate salt water. Except for a few salamanders that are viviparous they are oviparous and are compelled to breed in water, because their eggs are not adapted to develop in dry conditions. They have a smooth, moist skin rich in gland cells, that serves as a respiratory surface and is rich in blood vessels. Scales are absent. Gills are always present in the tadpoles and may persist into adult life, but lungs are found in the adults.

In the main, amphibians cannot tolerate dry conditions and cannot, therefore, spread across deserts. They are most abundant in the tropics, decreasing rapidly towards the arctic circle, with a northern limit that roughly follows the fifty-eighth parallel in the eastern hemisphere and the fiftieth in the western.

The tortoises, terrapins, lizards and snakes belong to the Class Reptilia, from the Latin word *reptilis* = crawling; a name given to them because they crawl rather than walk.

Reptiles are completely adapted to life on land both as adults and in their embryonic development. The skin is dry and bears horny epidermal scales. Bony plates may also be present. Breathing is entirely by lungs. With a few exceptions they are oviparous. The eggs are large-yolked and encased in a leathery shell. In general they are retained within the body of the parent until the development of the young has proceeded to a greater or lesser extent, and then expelled on dry land and left to incubate in the sun. There is no larval (tadpole) stage as in the amphibians.

Reptiles are cosmopolitan, though they are absent from the poles and most abundant in the tropics.

The amphibians were the first vertebrates to emerge from the waters and take to the land. This they did during the Devonian period, a matter of some 300 million years ago. It was a period of seasonal droughts, and survival depended on the evolution of a new method of breathing. The problem was solved by the dipnoans, the so-called lung fishes, that inhabited the putrefying swamps. In this group, which today is represented only in equatorial America, Africa and Australia, the swim-bladder is in direct communication with the pharynx and has become converted into a lung. It enables *Ceratodus*, the barramundi of Queensland, to live in the foul water brought about by decaying vegetation, by periodically rising to the surface for air, and *Protopterus* of the Gran Chaco and *Lepidosiren* of the Upper Nile basin, to aestivate in the mud when the water in which they have been living dries up.

The structure of these dipnoan fishes shows a strong affinity to that of the amphibians, and though there are certain specializations, which suggest that they are slightly off the direct line, it is highly significant that the young of the dipnoans breathe by external gills like those of amphibian tadpoles.

The change from water to land necessitated other structural modifications. Fins designed for propelling a body through water had to be adapted into legs for creeping or crawling on land. The problem of dessication had to be solved; for a body once perpetually immersed in water now had to cope with constant sun and drying winds. Then, too, all the sense organs had to be re-organized.

It was altogether too much for one group of animals, and though it may be said that the amphibians colonized the land, their valiant attempt to conquer it failed. This failure was due in part to the fact that the fish-lung is not a very efficient organ, so that among amphibians much of the breathing has to be done through the moist skin; indeed, some of the smaller forms rely on it entirely and have lost their lungs. Above all, except in a few rare cases, the larvae of amphibians remain aquatic, and for the all-important purpose of breeding, therefore, the adults must have access to water. Thus an amphibian remains permanently tied to the water from which it emerged; one of nature's failures, little more than a specialized type of fish capable of walking on land.

It was left to the reptiles, that followed the amphibians

along the corridor of life, to complete the conquest of dry land. This they did by evolving a type of egg which could be laid on land. By means of a yolk sac on which the embryo feeds, an amnion, a liquid-filled sac that affords it protection against injury and dessication, and an allantois, rich in branching blood vessels, that serves it as a lung because the outer shell is porous and permits the passage of oxygen and carbon dioxide, the aquatic life-stage, so vital to the amphibians, is unecessary to the reptiles. The embryo develops directly and more perfectly to a permanent land existence which it assumes immediately on hatching.

Once emancipation from the water had been completed, for the 100 million years or so that we call the Mesozoic era, the reptiles dominated the earth and the sky above it. Among those early reptiles were the first bipeds, and it was out of the flying reptiles of the Jurassic period of 150 million years ago that the birds evolved.

But by the end of the Cretaceous period of 70 million years ago the great dinosaurs, those terrible lizards whose huge size captures the public imagination, had taken their last curtain call. To the question why, no certain answer can be given, and no single answer would suffice. The only certain thing is that the age of the reptiles was over, and with the coming of the Eocene period, that followed the Cretaceous, there began the age of the mammals culminating in man.

The days of giants are past, and the modern reptiles, from the huge ocean-going turtles and alligators of the Mississippi swamps to the tiny terrapins and harmless lizards that we keep in our vivaria, are no more than the insignificant survivors of a group that evolved towards the end of the Palaeozoic era of some 200 million years ago, and conquering every habitat held sway over land, water and air for 100 million years.

2

Frogs and Toads

≫≫≫≫≫≫≫≫≫≫≫≫≫≫≫≫≫≫≫≫≫≫≫≫≫≫≫≫≫≫

Frogs and toads of the Class Amphibia are referred to the Order Anura, from the Greek prefix *an-* = without, and the word *oura* = tail. They are so called because though they have tails in the tadpole stage, they lose them at metamorphosis, the change from tadpole to adult.

Frogs and toads are easily identified. Their hind legs are long and powerful and the toes webbed; their front legs are comparatively short and the toes are not webbed. As a result of this, in the water they are excellent swimmers, propelling themselves forward by alternate kicks which push the webbed toes against the water: on land they are excellent jumpers though the length of a frog-jump is often exaggerated and, even under good conditions, our native species cannot do more than a yard. Some foreign species may do more. The front legs are very little used in swimming; their function is mainly to support the head and trunk when the creature is at rest, and to break the force of the fall on landing from a jump.

Externally there is little to distinguish a toad from a frog. In general, however, the true toads are more squat than frogs. Then, too, they are more sedentary, mainly nocturnal, and walk or crawl rather than jump; at best they take only short hops. The skin both of frogs and toads contains glands that secrete an acrid fluid. It is not very effective and does no harm

27

on human skin unless it is broken. On mucous surfaces, such as the eye, however, it may produce inflammation, but this usually passes off harmlessly. The fluid cannot be squirted; it is exuded under pressure, and any dog or other animal that once takes a toad in its mouth will not do so a second time in a hurry.

As a result of this a toad may be allowed the run of the garden with a large flower-pot stood on its side, or some rockery stones piled up, to give it a retreat. In the garden toads will do nothing but good, for they have an insatiable appetite for wood lice, ants, beetles and other pests, which they will soon learn to take from between finger and thumb. There is a certain risk of losing them if they are not confined in a vivarium, but they have a remarkable homing instinct and time and time again they will return to some favoured spot. It is, of course, a wise precaution to block all escape holes in the fences.

Altogether naturalists recognize a very large number of species, which they have classified into fourteen families. In England only three species of frog (one of which is a new-comer) and two species of toad are found. It is best to keep them in an outdoor vivarium.

The common frog (*Rana temporaria temporaria*) is an ideal subject for the outdoor vivarium, for in nature it lives mainly in shady, damp situations never far from water. It has a wide range, extending from western Ireland to Japan, and is to be found in most suitable localities between these two countries, even at a height of 10,000 feet in the Alps.

The edible frog (*Rana esculenta*) is similar in appearance to the common frog, but may be distinguished from it by the presence of three lighter stripes on the back. In England it is local, and may be dying out. Of European origin some say that it was first introduced by the Romans, others during the Middle Ages by the monks for their Friday dinners. The first written record, however, dates the import to 1837. The female is rather bigger than the male.

Frogs and Toads

The marsh or laughing frog (*Rana ridibunda ridibunda*) is so called because in this country it is more or less confined to the Romney Marshes (Fig. 3). It dates only from 1935, when a Mr. E. P. Smith, of Stone-in-Oxney, liberated twelve specimens in his garden pond. They had arrived at University College, London from Debreczen in Hungary. Later in the year they escaped on to the marshes and colonized. It is the

Fig. 3. Marsh Frog (*Rana ridibunda ridibunda*) (vocal sacs distended)

largest of all European frogs, reaching a length of about five inches, and as much as a foot when outstretched. The female is even larger. Like most frogs it spends much of its time sprawled on the surface of the water with only its nose and eyes protruding. At the first sign of danger it quickly submerges and swims to cover. It is sometimes called the laughing frog on account of the loud quacking croak that it makes, accurately recorded in the throaty 'Brekekekex, koax, koax' of Aristophanes.

The common toad (*Bufo bufo bufo*) and the natterjack toad (*Bufo calamita*) are both widespread in Britain, but the common toad is not found in Ireland, and the natterjack only in the south-west, where it was introduced about the beginning of the nineteenth century (Fig. 4). On the whole, however, the common toad has a very wide range; for it extends across Europe from Norway southwards to north Africa, and eastwards across Siberia as far south as the Himalayas to China. Both species are very variable in colour, but can be distin-

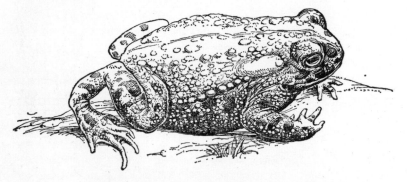

Fig. 4. Natterjack Toad (*Bufo calamita*)

guished from each other by the fact that the natterjack is much the smaller and has a yellowish or reddish stripe down the back. It can scarcely jump, but runs like a mouse. The origin of the popular name that has become attached to it is by no means certain. It is thought by some to be an easy corruption of the Anglo-Saxon *naedre* from the Icelandic *nadhr* = a snake, and by others of the Anglo-Saxon *atter* = poison. But the evidence for both is scanty and not very reliable, and perfectionists may prefer to reject the controvertible natterjack toad for the incontrovertible running toad. It does run.

Frogs and Toads

In this country frogs and toads begin to breed in early spring, though the marsh frog is a late starter and sometimes delays until July. Their breeding habits are identical, except that frogs deposit their spawn as a mass protected by a coat of albuminous jelly, but toads as a long, albuminous string (sometimes several feet long) festooned among the water plants.

Essentially frogs and toads are solitary and unsociable creatures. At the breeding season, however, they become highly gregarious and congregate in large numbers in shallow bodies of water. The male clasps the female from behind in an embrace that normally lasts for several days. Strange as it may appear, the fertilization of the eggs is external; for the male has no pairing organ. The embrace (properly called the amplexus) is in reality an excitable reflex action of the male, who discharges the sperms to fertilize the eggs as they emerge.

About a fortnight after the eggs have been deposited (though the length of time depends on the temperature) the larvae (tadpoles) wriggle from the albuminous covering into the surrounding water. They are fish-like, without limbs, with external gills and a swimming tail. At first they are very inactive and cling to the leaves of the water plants. Soon they begin to swim more freely, feeding on algae and refuse of various kinds. After a week or two a membrane grows over the external gills. Growth is now more rapid. Hind limbs bud from the body and gradually increase in size. Lungs develop, and the tadpole has to come to the surface of the water to breathe. About three months after hatching the front legs appear, the tadpole ceases to feed and its tail gradually decreases in size; for at this stage the tadpole absorbs its tail and utilizes it as nourishment. With the loss of the tail the metamorphosis is complete, and the young animal crawls out of the water, a tiny and brilliantly clean replica of the adult.

Our native frogs and toads are rather drab. For colour in the vivarium there is the green toad (*Bufo viridis viridis*) from southern Europe. Of the same genus as our two native toads, like them it is very variable in colour, but at its best it is light green with chocolate-brown blotches.

Far more colourful are the fire toads, which rarely grow to more than a couple of inches in length. There are two species suitable for the aqua-vivarium, both from Europe. The fire-bellied (*Bombina bombina*) and the yellow-bellied (*Bombina variegata variegata*). (Plate A, opposite.) The back is dark green, the underparts are mottled with orange and vermilion in the fire belly, with yellow in the yellow belly. In the young the brilliant colours are absent; they do not show until the animal is about a year old, and do not reach full intensity until the age of about three. Fire toads are active creatures, and though largely aquatic, do not always keep to the water.

Of similar size, but far less aquatic than the fire toads, and hardy enough to endure the average English winter in an outdoor vivarium (provided they can bury themselves several inches in well-drained soil) are the burrowing spade-foot toads, so called because they have horny, sharp-edged appendages, like small spades, underneath their feet. With these they burrow into the ground, working backwards at tremendous speed. Three species are found wild in Europe; *Pelobates fuscus fuscus* which ranges across the continent from Belgium to Persia, *Pelobates cultripes* which is found in Spain, the south of France and Morocco, and *Pelobates syriacus balcanicus* which is found in the Balkans, to Syria and Asia Minor. Of the three *P. f. fuscus* is the most usually imported. It lives happily in an indoor vivarium, though the fact that it is essentially nocturnal does not make it a good pet. Breeding takes place in April and May. The eggs are wound round submerged plants in strings about eighteen inches long, and though the adult male reaches a length of about two and a half inches and the female three and a quarter, the tadpoles sometimes reach a length of seven inches from head to tail. These toads are sometimes called garlic toads, because when frightened they exude a secretion that smells strongly of garlic.

32

Plate A
FROGS and TOADS
European Tree Frog *(Hyla arborea arborea)*
Agile Frog *(Rana dalmatina)*
Midwife Toad *(Alytes obstetricans obstetricans)*
Yellow-bellied Toad *(Bombina variegata variegata)*

Plate B

NEWTS and SALAMANDERS

European Salamander *(Salamandra salamandra salamandra)*
Black Salamander *(Salamandra atra)*
Alpine Newt ♂ & ♀ *(Triturus alpestris alpestris)*
Marbled Newt ♂ & ♀ *(Triturus marmoratus marmoratus)*

Frogs and Toads

A close relation of the fire toads is the painted frog (*Discoglossus pictus pictus*) that ranges from the Spanish peninsula and southern France, across Sicily and Malta to north-west Africa. It reaches a length of about two and a half inches, and a larger form, *Discoglossus pictus sardus*, is found in Sardinia and Corsica and their neighbouring islands. It will live very comfortably in an aqua-vivarium at room temperature; for it does not resent captivity; it feeds readily, is active by day and night, and quite content to sit for long hours on the bottom with only its head above the water-surface. It has a soft croak. The coloration is very variable. Dark brown patches, with or without a light edging, occur on a background that varies from reddish or brownish red to yellowish brown or grey. The underparts are ivory-white which are sometimes plain and sometimes speckled brown.

The agile frog (*Rana dalmatina*) which is found in southern central Europe northwards to Denmark, and in western Asia, also makes a good pet. (Plate A, facing p. 32.) It must, however, be given a very large vivarium with frequent changes of plants and moss; for in nature it frequents deciduous woodlands and meadows, often a long way from water, thereby contradicting Goethe's 'There are not frogs wherever there is water; but wherever there are frogs, water will be found.' (*Sprüche in Prosa*). It is characterized by a very slender body and extremely long hind legs that enable it to jump as much as six feet. The general colour is light brown with or without a few dark speckles, and a large brownish black patch in the neighbourhood of the ear. The underparts are white or yellowish white usually unmarked. Males reach a length of about two and a half inches; females about three and a quarter inches.

The field frog (*Rana arvalis arvalis*) shares much the same range as the agile frog. It favours marshy fields and moors in low-lying country, and for this reason it is sometimes called the moor frog. Like the agile frog it has a slender body and long hind legs, but neither is so slender nor so long as in the agile frog, and it is a rather larger creature that is darker in colour. The general colour is brown, usually with dark brown or black patches and always with a large dark patch in the neighbourhood of the ear, and sometimes a light-coloured stripe down the back. The underparts are yellowish white and unmarked. During the breeding season the male sometimes develops a lavender-blue throat. Very pretty.

The midwife toad (*Alytes obstetricans obstetricans*) is rather sombre of colour, but has much to recommend it as an inmate of the vivarium. (Plate A, facing p.32.) It is small (two inches is an average length), has a musical croak, not unlike a tiny bell, and an unusual breeding habit. A string of some forty eggs, instead of being festooned about the water plants, are wound by the male about his thighs and back legs. When the eggs are ready to hatch (a matter of two or three weeks) he takes them to the nearest pond where the completely-formed tadpoles break out into the water, and the male wipes off the empty egg band.

This method of breeding is, of course, one of nature's ways to ensure the continuation of the species. It is vital when the species deposits only a comparatively few eggs. In the Surinam toad (*Pipa pipa*) from the north-east of South America, this method of breeding is even more pronounced; for at breeding time the male presses the eggs on to the back of the female, where they sink into little pockets in the skin. Here they remain, not only until the tadpoles hatch, but until they metamorphose. In this species the body is large (six to seven and a half inches is an average length) and flat, and the head is small and triangular. The webbing between the toes of the hind legs is large, and the tips of the toes of the front legs are star shaped.

More suited to the aquarium than to the aqua-vivarium, because it never leaves the water, is *Xenopus laevis*, which some classify as a toad and others as a frog. Either way it is particularly well known in this country as a laboratory pet which accurately predicts whether a woman is pregnant or not. In nature it is found in tropical Africa. In consequence it flourishes best in a temperature of sixty-five degrees to seventy degrees Fahrenheit, but it will live quite well at a temperature in the fifties.

By far the most charming creatures of the group, however, are the small tree frogs, which, by virtue of toes expanded into rounded adhesive discs, are able to cling to swaying leaves and, in captivity, even to the vertical sides of a vivarium.

The American tree frog (*Hyla versicolor versicolor*) is hardy enough to live at room temperature, but the Florida tree frog (*Hyla gratiosa gratiosa*), sometimes called the barking tree frog as its croak is a deep, hollow bark, which is grass-green with black blotches, and White's tree frog (*Hyla coerulea*) from Australia, which is bright green spotted white on its sides, need a vivarium heated to a temperature of sixty degrees to seventy degrees Fahrenheit.

The European or common tree frog (*Hyla arborea arborea*) is the only member of the genus that is native to Europe. (Plate A, facing p. 32.) It is much admired by all who meet with it on the French and Italian rivieras.

In the spring the frogs come out of hibernation and assemble in thousands, guided by the sharp loud call of the males, to which the females reply in a comparatively small voice. After several days spent in rhythmic declamations, the frogs collect near ponds and tanks and drop from the trees into the water, where the females each deposit some 800 to 1,000 eggs in a few yellow brown clumps.

When producing his call, the male inflates the skin of his throat like a balloon, and the air is driven alternatively from it into the lungs and back again over the vocal chords, which vibrate to produce a loud 'wharr, biz!', remarkably loud for such a small animal.

The back of the frog is a bright grass-green; the underparts are yellowish with a rosy tinge on the thighs. Occasionally the colour changes to a brownish purple, but returns after a day or two to its normal bright green. A great rarity is a

35

blue variety, the blue as beautiful as that of the forget-me-not or the finest turquoise. These blue frogs are sometimes to be bought in pet shops, and it is often thought that they are artificially coloured. This, however, is not so. The blue is produced by a peculiar reflection of the light from minute colourless particles, without the help of any blue-coloured substance.

These little frogs, which the French call *reinettes*, are quite easy to keep, and flourish well in a vivarium at room temperature, but dampness is essential for them. Due to the erroneous belief that they can foretell the weather, they are often kept in glass containers so small as to amount to cruelty. They reach a maximum length of about two inches.

Since in nature tree frogs are entirely arboreal, and they come down from the trees only to breed, their vivarium must be furnished with some leafy branches for them to rest on. Growing plants, such as aspidistra and ferns, may also be included.

Amphibians are surprisingly defenceless, and they rely almost entirely on concealment and a coloration that camouflages them when in their normal surroundings. Many of the tree frogs, however, have developed the method of protection that is known to naturalists as flash-colouring. The vivid green colour of these frogs, very suited to blend with the leaves of the trees which they inhabit, is interrupted by splashes of vivid yellow or red in the *axillae*. As a result, when the frog leaps from branch to branch these colours appear as bright flashes, that are eclipsed the moment that the frog resumes its resting position. The enemy in pursuit is temporarily dazzled by the sudden and unexpected display of colour, just as the human eye is temporarily blinded when the press photographer releases his flash and opens the shutter of his camera. In a split second the frog has vaulted on to a leaf, caught hold of it with his adhesive toe-discs, and demurely sits there indistinguishable from his background, because the pursuer, who has been following the flashes of colour, has had to keep his eyes a little ahead of his prey and now has to bring them back and search for something that has faded into immobility.

In the widest sense of the word, frogs and toads are carnivorous; that is to say they are eaters of animal rather than vegetable foods. In the wild, earthworms, insects, insect larvae and spiders are their normal diet. In captivity they may be offered small slugs, gentles, mealworms, and the like. Flies are much appreciated, but as in modern homes most flies are likely to have been in contact with poison sprays, it is safer to offer small pieces of meat dangled in front of them on a piece of black twine.

Because the teeth of frogs and toads are at best feeble, and some species are toothless, the protrusibility of the tongue is an important method of obtaining food. In most species it is attached anteriorly, and normally lies with its tip turned backwards in the mouth. When an insect passes within striking distance, the tongue is flipped out to make contact, and because the tip of the tongue as it passes over the palate receives a sticky substance secreted by the mouth, any object that it touches adheres to it. A reverse flip and the food is drawn into the mouth with the tongue and quickly gulped down. The formation of the tongue, however, varies with the species and in the pipids there is none.

Frogs and toads tend to snap at any moving object within range. It is an unfortunate characteristic that has resulted in premature death for thousands of edible frogs. In France frogs are farmed for the market (*grenouilles de parc*) but thousands are taken in the wild (*grenouilles de pêche*). The fishermen go out at night with a powerful lamp and a rod, at the end of which a piece of red cloth dangles from a line. The frogs are attracted by the light and snap at the cloth. A quick hand and a large bag completes the capture.

The common frog takes its place besides the edible frog as a table delicacy, although experienced diners tell us that its flesh is not so tasty. In America the bull frog (*Rana catesbiana*)

37

finds its way to the table. Small wonder when young ducklings are among its favourite foods. The American bull frog reaches a length of about seven inches. It is found nearly everywhere in the eastern United States and extends westwards as far as Wisconsin and Nebraska and southwards to Mexico. It has been introduced into California and British Columbia. Essentially aquatic, it lives in ponds also in running water, and as well as young ducklings it takes small fish, frogs and elvers, even butterflies.

Bull frogs, so called because they have a low-pitched croak that resembles the lowing of cattle, are greedy creatures. The Indian bull frog (*Rana tigrina*) that inhabits the marshes of India, Ceylon and south-east Asia, has been known to gulp down several small chicks in quick succession, and the African bull frog (*Rana adspersa*) found in southern Africa and northwards as far as the White Nile, eats large quantities of young rats, mice, frogs and other small creatures. It lives quite comfortably in a vivarium at a temperature of about seventy degrees Fahrenheit, and does not resent being handled. In colour it is olive-green on the back, shading to ivory-white on the underparts; the raised folds of skin on the back and lower sides are ivory to yellow in colour. It is mainly terrestrial. In the wild it spends its days buried in the ground and its nights in hunting for food, while itself is hunted for by the natives, who consider its flesh a great delicacy.

The Englishman is more conservative in matters that concern his stomacn, and frogs' legs rarely find a place on the menus of London hotels and restaurants. Many years ago they did, but there was no demand for them until an enterprising chef attached a romantic name to the dish; the demand died down when the truth leaked out, though it lingers on at a few expensive eating places.

3

Newts and Salamanders

❯❯

Newts (sometimes called efts) and salamanders of the Class Amphibia are referred to the Order Urodela from the Greek words *oura* = a tail and *delo* = to show. They are so called because, unlike as in their cousins the frogs and toads, their tail persists throughout life and is used in progression both on land and in water.

Newts and salamanders are lizard-like in appearance with fore and hind legs of about equal length, provided with toes, and relatively feeble. They do little more than keep the belly clear of the ground when the creature is moving: the legs may move freely, but the body is still thrown into sinuous curves which push it forward on the legs supporting it. The vertebral column is long. External as well as internal gills may persist in the adult, and, if they do, the lungs tend to atrophy. The skin is soft and moist. The eyesight and sense of smell are good. The mouth is large and furnished with minute teeth on both jaws (in some species there are additional teeth on the palate) and a small and pad-like tongue is situated anteriorly and more or less secured to the floor of the mouth all round. There is only a limited flexibility of the tongue at the sides: the complete protrusion seen when newts swallow bulky food on land, is effected by a forward and outward movement of the floor of the mouth itself.

The voice is small, and the squeaking sound which newts

sometimes make, particularly when roughly handled, is the result of the sudden expulsion of air from the lungs.

Superficially newts and salamanders are much alike, and American workers make little attempt to distinguish one from the other: they take the view that a newt is only a particular kind of salamander. In fact, the difference between the newts and salamanders is not great, but the salamanders are terrestrial, though they require moisture as well as shade for their well-being, and they are nocturnal in their habits. The newts are more or less aquatic, and for this reason are sometimes called water-salamanders. If kept indoors they should be housed in an aqua-vivarium, so that they may enter or leave the water at will. Also a newt has a slimmer body than a salamander; it terminates in a strongly compressed tail whereas that of the salamander is rounded. Finally, newts, but not salamanders, periodically shed their skins. In captivity the action is most often performed after a change of water. The old skin begins to break at the mouth and is peeled away from the body in one piece. These casts float in the water in one piece, and as they remain perfect, even to the separate toes and wrinkles, until they disintegrate in the water or are eaten by the newt itself, they may be likened to ghosts.

No species of salamander is found in the British Isles, but three species of newt are: the crested newt, the common newt and the palmate newt. They are widespread and common except in Ireland where only the common newt is found; and the palmate newt, as it favours high ground (it has been taken at 3,000 feet) and acid soil, is not found in eastern England but is the dominant form in the west.

The crested or warty newt (*Triturus cristatus cristatus*) is the largest newt found in the British Isles (Fig. 5). Normally it reaches a length of about five and a half to six inches, the female up to six and a half inches and occasionally as much as seven inches or slightly more. The male, when in breeding condition, displays a high, serrated crest along the back which dips sharply at the tail, and a pearl-coloured stripe along each side of the tail. The general colour is a deep brown with black spots; the underparts yellow or orange with black spots. The skin is warty, and when the newt is seized by a predator in its mouth it is invariably ejected immediately because under pressure the skin exudes a bitter secretion. As well as being found in the British Isles, it ranges across Europe from

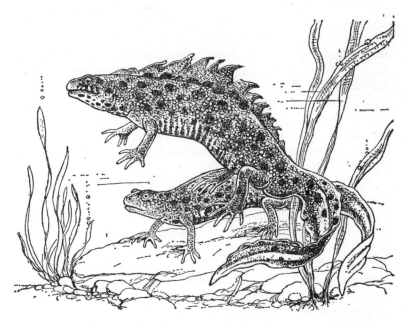

Fig. 5. Crested Newt (*Triturus cristatus cristatus*)
♂ above   ♀ below

France to the Urals, but is replaced in the valley of the Danube by *T. c. danubialis* and from the Crimea and Caucasus eastwards to Iran by *T. c. karelinii*, which has bigger spots and is more aquatic.

The common, or smooth, newt (*Triturus vulgaris vulgaris*) reaches a length of about four inches, the female rather less. The male, when in breeding condition, displays a wavy dorsal crest that continues onto the tail, and a pearl-coloured stripe along the lower edge. The general colour is brown to olive, with darker spots; the underparts are whitish to pink with black spots that are large in the male and small in the female. It is widespread across Europe, except the far north, and extends into Asia Minor.

The palmate newt (*Triturus helveticus helveticus*) is the smallest of the three species found in the British Isles. The male rarely exceeds a length of three inches, the female is only slightly larger. The male, when in breeding condition, displays a low, striped crest along the back, and a thread-like extension to the tail. The general colour is brown to olive-brown with dark spots; the underparts are whitish with a median band of light orange. The feet are webbed. A smaller sub-species, *T. h. sequeirai*, is found in northern Spain and Portugal, and has been taken in the Pyrenees at over 5,000 feet.

Breeding takes place from spring to midsummer, in water. The male courts the female by contortions of the body and archings of the tail, the tip of which vibrates. The male deposits a spermatophore which is taken up by the female into her cloaca. The spermatozoa pass into her oviduct to fertilize the eggs, and about a week later she deposits the eggs. By means of her hind legs the female bends the leaf of a water plant to form a pocket, into which a single egg is deposited by virtue of the jelly-like substance that encases it.

The larvae (tadpoles) hatch out in about ten days. They are carnivorous and feed on aquatic animals such as small water fleas (*Daphnia* and *Cyclops*). But, of course, as the tadpoles grow they require larger and larger food such as *Tubifex*, *Enchytraeus* and bloodworms, and if it is not available the weaker ones go to the wall. Metamorphosis takes about three or four months, but late tadpoles overwinter in the water. Maturity is reached in about three or four years.

Our three native species do not make ideal pets. The chief reason is that when the breeding season is over they tend to leave the water and retire to some permanently moist spot on land, there to sink into hibernation until the following spring. Then, too, with the possible exception of the crested newt, the British species, like the British species of frogs and toads, are rather drab.

A more colourful species, and one that is far more amenable to life in captivity than any of our native species, is the marbled newt (*Triturus marmoratus marmoratus*) that occurs in southern Europe from Portugal, through Spain, to central and southern France. (Plate B, facing p. 33.) The general colour is grass- to olive-green with black marbling; the underparts shade from grey to a deep brown with white or black spots. The male, when in breeding condition, develops a dorsal crest that continues onto the tail; it is marked with black and yellow, vertical stripes. In the wild it reaches a length of about seven and a half inches, but in captivity about six inches appears to be average. A smaller form, *T. m. pygmaeus*, is to be found in the south of the Iberian peninsula and through southern and central France. It has crossed with the crested newt to form a number of distinct colour races in which shades of green predominate. The marbled newt and its varieties are quite hardy and will live in an aqua-vivarium at room temperature, but should not be kept with smaller species.

So also will the Japanese, or fire-bellied, newt (*Cynops pyrrhogaster*) from Japan and the north-east of China. It is an attractive creature that reaches a length of about four inches. The back is dark, almost black; the underparts are bright red blotched with black. The male does not develop a nuptial crest, but, at the breeding season, the red in his tail diminishes.

A great favourite among vivarium keepers is the alpine newt (*Triturus alpestris alpestris*) so called because it inhabits the mountainous regions of southern Europe, from central Spain across the Pyrenees and Alps to northern Greece. (Plate B, facing p. 33). It is quite small; the male rarely exceeds a length of three and a quarter inches, the female four and a half inches. The coloration is very variable. The most attractive specimens are a dark purplish grey with black mottling; the underparts are orange-yellow to deep orange with black spots on the throat. The sides are sometimes mottled with white. The eyes are a golden yellow. The male, when in breeding condition, develops a low, smooth crest, yellow in colour with black, vertical stripes and spots. The female is less colourful, being grey or brownish with a darker marbled pattern. In the mountains the summer is too short for the larva to develop so neoteny, therefore, commonly occurs; that is, it persists as a larva with its sex organs fully developed and, as in the better known axolotl (*see* p. 45), it is capable of breeding in its juvenile form.

For the large aqua-vivarium an interesting pet is the Spanish newt (*Pleurodeles waltl*) that is found in Morocco and the southern and western parts of the Iberian peninsula. It is also known as the ribbed newt on account of the large number of vertebrae with rib joints, the pointed ends of which sometimes pierce the skin of the sides. For a newt it is exceptionally large; specimens average from six to eight inches in length and some have been found no less than sixteen inches long. It should not be kept with smaller species. The general colour is olive-grey and greenish, lightening to yellowish on the underparts, the whole body marked with irregular patches. In the male the tail is longer than in the female, and, at the breeding season, the male develops pads on the under side of the fore legs. He tends towards mating at any sudden change of temperature. The female deposits the eggs in clusters on stones or water plants.

Normally newts take to the water at the breeding season and leave it in late-summer, often travelling far from water. They hibernate under stones and logs, where they may be mistaken for lizards. Some (*e.g.* the crested newt), however, are more aquatic and remain longer in the water, sometimes remaining in it for the whole year, and hibernating at the bottom of the pond.

Newts and Salamanders

Mention must be made of the axolotl, although it lives entirely in water and is, therefore, more suited to the aquarium (which need not be heated) than either the vivarium or more exactly the aqua-vivarium. It is native to the western states of the U.S.A., and to Mexico where it is much esteemed as a table delicacy. It was first brought to Europe by the Spanish *conquistadores* and long thought to be a distinct species. But exactly a century ago as we write (in 1865 that is) some specimens in the Jardins des Plantes, in Paris, lost their gills and climbed out of the water. It was then learnt that, in fact, the axolotl is not a species but the larval stage of a salamander, first thought to be the tiger salamander (*Amblystoma tigrinum*) but now thought to be the Mexican salamander (*A. mexicanum*) that remains in the water and breathes by means of external, branched gills.

That they are capable of breeding in juvenile form is now well known, and in captivity it is quite easy to induce a pair to breed by keeping them first in a small aquarium without plants and then moving them to a large aquarium that is well stocked with submerged plants. The phenomenon is known as paedogenesis. They can also be induced to develop into adults either by keeping them under gradually drier conditions, or, more scientifically, by means of systematic doses of thyroid-gland extract.

Axolotls taken from the wild are black with or without lighter spots, but a more handsome albino form with red eyes and gill filaments has been developed in domestication. The male reaches a length of about six to nine inches, the female rather more. Its name, unchanged since stout Cortez stared at the Pacific silent upon a peak in Darien, is the Aztec for water-servant.

We come to the salamanders. That man once thought they lived in fire, as man once thought toads lived encased in rocks or lumps of coal, is a story that was exploded nearly 2,000 years ago. In his *Natural History* (x, 67 and xxix, 4) the elder Pliny (A.D. 23–79) tells us that he tried the experiment once, only to find, as he expected, that the salamander was burnt to a powder. The salamander that has given its name to the kitchen utensil that is used for browning omelettes was, in fact, a mythical lizard-like monster that was supposed to be able to live in fire, as the mythical phoenix was supposed to rise from its own ashes. It was taken up by Paracelsus (A.D. 1493–1541) the Swiss physician and naturalist as the name of the elemental beings who inhabited fire, as gnomes inhabited the earth, sylphs the air, and nymphs the water. We find it again in the Rosicrucian Doctrine of Spirits from where Alexander Pope borrowed also the notion that the spirits were the souls of the dead who protected those who had been their friends on earth. Thus we read in the first canto (lines 57–60) of the 1714 version of the heroi-comical *The Rape of the Lock*:

> *For when the fair in all their pride expire,*
> *To their first elements their souls retire:*
> *The sprites of fiery termagants in flame*
> *Mount up, and take a salamander's name.*

Although the three newts that are native to this country are referred by taxonomists to the Family Salamandridae, as we have said above, no true salamander is found wild in the British Isles.

In fact, very few salamanders are to be found even in captivity, because the majority of them are not very amenable to domestication. In nature many of them inhabit the high mountains, 5,000 and more feet above sea level, and many will not survive unless they are given constant humidity and plenty of hiding places in a vivarium that is kept out of the sun and at a temperature below sixty-eight degrees Fahrenheit. Some are particular about their food: thus the spectacled salamander (*Salamandrina ter-digitata*) from the Ligurian slopes of the Apennines and the golden-striped salamander (*Chioglossa lusitanica*) from Portugal and north-west Spain, will take only live food. The tongue of the latter is fixed in front but free at the sides and back, and can be shot out with unerring aim to capture flies and other insects. It stalks its prey in the manner of a chameleon, and moves as fast as a lizard.

As a result, therefore, outside of a zoo, only two species of salamander are kept in this country, namely the spotted or European salamander (*Salamandra salamandra salamandra*) and the black or alpine salamander (*Salamandra atra*). (Plate B, facing p. 33.) Both are fairly easy to keep in a moist vivarium and though *S. s. salamandra* is reputed to live a long time, *S. atra* is said to be short-lived when in captivity.

S. s. salamandra is a very handsome creature with a smooth, black skin marked with lemon-yellow, golden or orange coloured patches. The eyes are brown; the body plump; there is a large parotid gland near the ear and a row of warts on each side of the body. It reaches a length of about eight inches. It is widespread in the hilly and mountainous districts of central and southern Europe. A number of sub-species are known, of which the striped salamander (*Salamandra salamandra quadrivirgata*) is the one most usually imported. It differs from the type by the yellow markings on the body being joined to form two stripes along the back.

S. atra is found in the European Alps as far south as Albania. At heights about 2,500 feet it replaces *S. s. salamandra* and continues up to 9,000 feet and more. The colour is a uniform shiny black, unmarked, and the eyes are black too. Apart from this and a slimmer and shorter body (six inches is an average length) it is much the same as *S. s. salamandra*, with a large parotid gland near the ear and a row of warts on each side of the body.

In the wild salamanders hibernate from October to March in ditches, under logs or stones, or among rocks. They breed from spring to summer. The male climbs clumsily on the back of the female and wraps his front legs around her. The spermatophores that he deposits are taken up by the female into her cloaca. She is capable of retaining the spermatozoa in her body for a long time, thus delaying fertilization of the egg and postponing birth until the end of the summer, or even to the following spring.

S. s. salamandra deposits her larvae while squatting in shallow water. At birth the young are about an inch long with external gills. They feed in the same way as newt-tadpoles (*see* p. 42), metamorphosing at about four months and leaving the water when about two inches long.

In *S. atra* each oviduct contains some twenty eggs, but only the first develops: the others form a shapeless mass on which the embryos feed. As a result of this the salamander is independent of water and deposits two fully developed larvae on land.

Like frogs and toads, newts and salamanders are carnivorous in the widest sense of the word. They eat any small living animals of suitable size, such as flies and other insects, small earthworms, wood-lice, tadpoles and small fish. In captivity, care should be taken to avoid giving them insects that have been in contact with toxic sprays. Small pieces of meat make an excellent substitute.

Food is taken with a quick snap of the mouth. Newts eat on land as well as in the water; salamanders eat only on land, and, indeed, are notoriously such poor performers in the water that couples that get into difficulties when breeding sometimes drown.

Plate C
TORTOISES and TERRAPINS
Leopard Tortoise *(Testudo pardalis)*
Carolina Box Tortoise *(Terrapene carolina carolina)*
Elegant Terrapin *(Pseudemys scripta elegans)*
European Pond Tortoise *(Emys orbicularis)*
Ornate Terrapin *(Pseudemys ornata)*

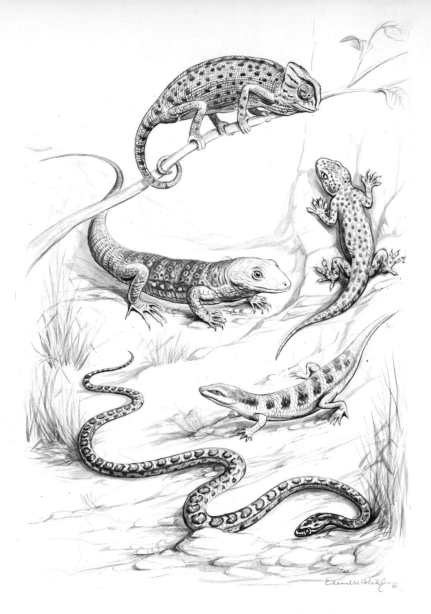

Plate D

LIZARDS and SNAKES
  Common Chameleon *(Chamaeleo chamaeleon chamaeleon)*
                    Great House Gecko *(Gecko gekko)*
  Eyed Lizard *(Lacerta lepida lepida)*
                    Sand Skink *(Scincus scincus)*
  Leopard Snake *(Elaphe situla)*

4

Tortoises and Terrapins

꧅꧅꧅꧅꧅꧅꧅꧅꧅꧅꧅꧅꧅꧅꧅꧅꧅꧅꧅꧅꧅꧅꧅꧅꧅꧅꧅

Tortoises and terrapins of the Class Reptilia are referred to the Order Chelonia, from the Greek word *chelone* = a tortoise. The turtles also belong to this Order, but, as they are marine species and cannot, therefore, be kept in a vivarium, they are passed over in this book, and left to the gormandizing aldermen.

Superficially all three forms—tortoises, terrapins and turtles—are very much alike: the trunk is relatively short and broad and protected by a dorsal shell (known as the carapace) and a ventral shell (known as the plastron). They are sensitive organs and to paint them—as some have been known to—is to condemn the creature to a slow and painful death; to carve on them is even more to be condemned. Typically the carapace and plastron are composed of bony plates overlaid by large horny epidermal shields—the tortoiseshell of commerce. The carapace and plastron are joined at the sides, either by a rigid bony union or by a flexible cartilaginous one, only leaving apertures for the head, tail and legs. The carapace is convex to a greater or lesser degree; the plastron is concave in the male, flat in the female. The jaws are strong, but they lack teeth which are replaced by a horny bill or beak. The eyesight is keen; the hearing, at least in most species, is no more than fair; only hissing noises are made.

In practice the three forms are not difficult to distinguish. Tortoises are essentially terrestrial though a few species enter

D   49

shallow water to bathe; the carapace is strongly arched; the toes are bound together by the skin, and only the strong horny nails are apparent; with a few exceptions they are strictly vegetarian. Terrapins live in fresh water and marshes (they are, therefore, sometimes called pond tortoises); the carapace is weakly arched; the toes are divided, partly webbed and furnished with long sharp claws; for they are carnivorous and in the wild feed mainly on small fish, tadpoles, crustaceans, and even small birds and mammals. Turtles, as we have pointed out, are marine, and are easily set apart from tortoises and terrapins; for their forelegs are replaced by paddle-like flippers.

Chelonians are oviparous. The two sexes show a number of external differences. We have already mentioned the difference in the plastron. Males have a more powerful head; a thicker base to a rather longer tail than females; and in some species the male is better coloured and somewhat smaller. Fertilization of the eggs is internal. The female digs a hole about five inches deep in the ground, the eggs are deposited in it, covered with earth or vegetation and left for the sun to hatch. The eggs are most usually spherical, with a white chalky shell. Those that are laid by pet tortoises in captivity are not worth troubling with. If no male is present they are unlikely to be fertile. If a male is present and the eggs are fertile, the English sun is rarely warm enough to hatch them. They have to be dug up and reburied in fine damp sand (taking the precaution to retain them in the same position) and kept in a garden frame or greenhouse at a day temperature of about eighty degrees Fahrenheit. Even then there is the difficulty of raising the young. When newly hatched a tortoise is about the size of a florin and has a soft shell, like putty. It has to be carefully looked after until the shell hardens and is about three inches long.

No tortoise is native to the British Isles. The nearest circle the Mediterranean, where six species and sub-species are to be found.

Tortoises and Terrapins

Testudo graeca graeca, the spur-thighed Mediterranean tortoise, is the best known and most frequently imported. It is common, but not abundant, along the African coast from Cyrenica to Morocco, and extends into southern Spain. Along the European coast, from Spain, through France, Italy and the Balkans to Asia Minor and Syria it is replaced by the sub-species *Testudo graeca ibera*. The carapace is yellowish or olive. The sutures of the shields are black, and the shields themselves marked with dark brown to black blotches, those on the marginal shields are triangular in shape. The scales on the front part of the forelegs are large, and arranged in four rows lengthwise; on the hindlegs scales are confined to the heels. There is a large conical tubercle on the back of the thigh. The plastron of the male is slightly movable from behind.

The metropolis of *Testudo hermanni hermanni*, Hermann's tortoise, more usually known as the Greek tortoise, is the Balkan peninsula, but it extends into Italy and to the islands of Sicily and Corsica; in Sardinia and the Balearic Islands, as well as along the European coast, from southern France to Spain, its place is taken by the sub-species *Testudo hermanni robertmertensi*. In good specimens the shields of the carapace are coal black spectacularly edged with yellow. More often, however, the coloration is subdued and it resembles *T. graeca*. It may be distinguished by a carapace that is smoother and has a more polished appearance, and a rigid plastron; by the absence of tubercles on the thighs and the presence of a horny spur at the end of the tail.

Testudo marginata, the marginated tortoise, is found in southern Greece and is, therefore, more properly the Greek tortoise than either of the two species already mentioned. In general it is rather like them, at least when young, but may be set apart from them by reason of the four or five rows of large, overlapping scales down the front of the forelegs, by the absence of tubercles on the thighs and a spur at the end of the tail.

51

Tortoises and Terrapins

Testudo horsefieldii, Horsefield's tortoise, ranges from the Volga and the Russian province of Samara, across the Kirghiz Steppe and through Turkistan and Afghanistan, to north-west India. Not unexpectedly, therefore, it is less rarely imported than the three foregoing species. Although it has a spur at the end of its tail and small tubercles on its thighs, it is easily distinguished from the other forms by virtue of only four claws, instead of five, on each of its feet.

The tortoises that we have mentioned are all fairly small, averaging a length of from eight to twelve inches. They are commonly known as the European or Mediterranean tortoises, on account of their distribution in the wild. Brought to England they are quite hardy and may be kept in an outdoor vivarium, provided, of course, they are given adequate shelter against bad spells of weather in the summer months, and arrangements are made for them to hibernate in the cold months.

Here, in the outdoor vivarium, they may be accompanied by the box tortoises (*Terrapene* species) from North America. They are true tortoises whose chief characteristics are a strongly-arched (noticeably keeled in young specimens) carapace, clawed and webbed toes (which has led naturalists to believe that they are terrapins slowly returning to complete land life), and a bilobed plastron, attached to the carapace by a ligament, and which can be raised to close the shell completely. The male may be distinguished from the female by a longer tail, and by the posterior lobe of the plastron which is concave in males and flat in females.

Several species of *Terrapene* have been classified, but those most usually imported into Great Britain are the Carolina (*Terrapene carolina carolina*) (Plate C, facing p. 48) and the ornate or painted (*Terrapene ornata*). The carapace of the former is dark brown with yellowish spots and radiating dashes; it is strongly arched and the keel, usually seen only in young specimens, persists in the adults. A noticeable sex distinction is the eye which is red in the male, brown in the female. The carapace of the latter is reddish-brown, and though otherwise similarly marked to that of its congener, may be distinguished from it by a less arched carapace that lacks a keel. The colour of the eye is no guide to sex. In the wild it ranges across the central and eastern states of the U.S.A., from the Dakotas to Texas. Both species are on the small size, averaging five or six inches in length.

An outdoor vivarium for the hardy tortoises need be nothing elaborate; a very low wall is enough to restrict them, and there is no need to dig a pond. A shallow pan of water, sunk to the rim in the ground, is ample. The *Testudo* species require water only for drinking, and though the *Terrapene* species swim well, and in the wild will often make for water to escape an enemy, normally they remain on land with occasional spells of lying in shallow water.

Ideally the vivarium should be in a sunny position, enclosing a stretch of lawn, some low-growing shrubs to furnish shade, and a rain- and draught-proof hutch to provide shelter when it rains and in which the tortoises can sleep at nights.

About October the hardy tortoises go into hibernation, sooner or later according to the vagaries of the thermometer. In the wild they bury themselves in the ground until the warmer weather comes. Our garden soils are usually too hard for this, but if a tortoise does go to ground the spot should be marked to avoid disturbing it. Rather than allow tortoises to go to ground it is better to move them to winter quarters. Again nothing elaborate is necessary. The tortoise should be placed in a box of dry leaves, crumpled newspaper, or chopped hay or straw, covered with a loose-fitting lid, and stored (well away from draughts) in a cold but dry, frost-proof garden shed or unheated room in the house. A garage, on account of petrol fumes, is not the place for a hibernating tortoise, nor is a cellar because it is usually too damp. Although normally a wooden or cardboard box is satisfactory, if there is any risk from rats, as in a garden shed, the box should be a metal one with a close-fitting lid punctured for air.

If the winter is a mild one, it is as well to take an occasional look at any tortoise in hibernation, with the warning that on no account should it be disturbed. If it is found that the tortoise is awake, the best plan is to move it to a colder place at once, in the hope that it will return to hibernation without delay; if, however, it appears that unnoticed it has been awake for some time, it will be necessary to give it food and water for not less than a fortnight before moving it to a colder place. The reason is that the nourishment stored by the tortoise against hibernation will last the hibernating period only if it is not drawn on more than is absolutely necessary.

Reptiles, amphibians and fishes are very often referred to (even by those who should know better) as cold-blooded creatures. It is not such a precise definition as one might wish. More correctly they are poikilothermic, because their blood temperature varies with that of the surrounding air or water in which they live. It follows, therefore, that in the polar regions, if any were there, they would be almost continuously asleep; in the temperate zones they spend half their lives in hibernation; in warm countries, where the thermometer may rise to one hundred degrees Fahrenheit or more, they are more warm blooded than man himself whose blood temperature, within narrow limits, is maintained at a uniform ninety-eight point four degrees. It is only in these climes that they become active enough for a life of competition.

Asia, Africa and tropical America can show a large number of different species. The best known, due in part to its huge size (fifty-eight inches) and in part to the publicity that it has received through the work of Charles Darwin, is *Testudo elephantopus*, the giant tortoise of the Galapagos Islands, where at one time, if no longer, fourteen different races could be recognized.

Many of the smaller tortoises from the tropics are imported by dealers for sale as garden pets. During the summer months they may be kept in an outdoor vivarium, but it is important to remember that alternative accommodation must be available for them. They require a temperature between sixty-five degrees and seventy-five degrees Fahrenheit (depending on the species) and to this they must be moved in the autumn, even in the summer if there is a sudden cold spell, not unusual in the erratic British climate. Ideally, these tortoises from the tropics should be kept in an outdoor vivarium whose surrounding wall encloses a greenhouse heated to the required temperature all the year round. Thermostatic control is desirable.

The Brazilian giant tortoise (*Testudo denticulata* syn. *tabulata*) from the equatorial jungles of South America is basically yellow in colour, but obscured by brown pigmentation, and, in fact, young specimens are brown all over. The scales on the forelegs are yellow, deepening with age to orange to red. The head is orange. By nature it is a forest dweller accustomed to partial, even deep, shade, and with a dislike of direct sunlight. England should be no hardship to it. It should, however, be given some sunlight, as well as plenty of water (not only for drinking but for bathing) and plenty of room because not only is it more active than most of its kind but it reaches a large size; specimens as much as two feet long have been recorded. It is comparatively hardy, but frosts are dangerous to it. It does not hibernate and requires a temperature of about sixty-five degrees Fahrenheit all the year round.

Also from America is the gopher tortoise (*Gopherus polyphemus*) from the pine forests and sandy dunes of the southern United States, from Texas to Florida and northwards to South Carolina. It reaches a length of about ten inches, and is rather drab of appearance being a dark brown all over. In the wild it digs a tunnel from twelve to eighteen feet long that ends in a small compartment in which it lives—one compartment, one tortoise. In captivity it shows no great inclination to burrow, but it must have access to cover; for by nature it

55

is nocturnal. The eggs are laid at the beginning of June, buried to a depth of about three or four inches in a sunny position. They are worth recovering because they make excellent eating. The unusual name derives from the French *gaufre* = a honeycomb. The name was given by the early French settlers in America to a number of local animals that honeycomb the ground by burrowing in it. It is not connected with the gopher-wood of which Noah's ark was directed to be built; that, if it ever was, was probably of cypress.

Everyone knows that, on account of its climate, the African continent is rich in reptiles. Apart, however, from some rare species that are exhibited at zoological gardens, only one species of tortoise, or more correctly two since a species from Madagascar must be accounted among the African fauna, are imported into England.

That from the mainland is the leopard tortoise (*Testudo pardalis*) aptly so named because its strongly arched carapace is dull yellow marked with black spots. (Plate C, facing p. 48.) It ranges across the whole continent south of the equator, but the majority of specimens brought to Europe come from Kenya, where it is taken in large quantities for its meat. The scales on the hind legs of the female are large. It grows to a large size, and in the wild specimens weighing as much as seventy-five pounds have been caught. Such an animal naturally needs a large enclosure and plenty of food and drinking water. It enjoys the sun, but shade should be available. It does not hibernate, and a winter temperature of seventy degrees Fahrenheit is necessary to keep it feeding.

The radiated tortoise (*Testudo radiata*) is native to Madagascar. It is quite a handsome creature with a black carapace and vivid orange or yellow lines radiating from the centre of each shield. The head and legs are yellow. It weighs up to about eighteen pounds and may reach a length of about fifteen inches.

The starred or elegant tortoise (*Testudo elegans*) from India and Ceylon, is similar in appearance to the radiated tortoise, from Madagascar, but smaller (Fig. 6). It rarely exceeds a length of eight inches. Neither it nor the radiated tortoise should ever be subjected to a temperature below sixty-five degrees Fahrenheit.

Tortoises are not difficult to feed. In the main they are vegetarian and will eat the left-overs from the kitchen, such as the outer leaves of cabbages, lettuces and Brussels sprouts, potato peelings and the like. Fruit is appreciated, but it need not be of the best quality. Strawberries, raspberries, tomatoes

Fig. 6. Starred Tortoise (*Testudo elegans*)

and other soft fruits that are over-ripe or have been spoiled for the table are quite good enough for them. They enjoy the skins of bananas even more than the fruit itself, and they are very partial to dandelions, marigolds and roses.

In addition box tortoises will eat earthworms, slugs and wood-lice, also small pieces of raw meat and white fish as alternatives.

Food must be offered in large quantities; for animals that hibernate have to eat in summer against the winter, and from time to time it should be sprinkled with crushed egg-shell or cuttle-fish to provide them with calcium for strong shell-growth. Clean water should be available to them at all times. They drink a lot.

The word tortoise derives from the Latin *tortus* the past particle of *torqueo* = to twist, so named on account of its twisted feet. The word terrapin—because we must now turn our attention to this group—is believed a corruption of the Algonkin *toarebe* = a tortoise. Originally the name was attached to the diamond back (*Malaclemys terrapin*) that inhabits the brackish marshes of the Atlantic coast of North America, from Rhode Island to the Gulf of Mexico. Its flesh is excellent eating and it is reared in farms (called crawls) where it is fattened for the market on shrimps, clams and other shellfish. By a logical extension, later the name became attached to similar forms (*e.g. Chrysemys* species) native of North America. Today it is indifferently used, at all events in England, of all chelonians that live in fresh water and marshes, as opposed to those that are marine (turtles) and those that are terrestrial (tortoises).

An outdoor vivarium for terrapins may be built in the same way as one for tortoises; in fact the two forms may share the same enclosure, but since terrapins are more active and more accomplished climbers than tortoises the surrounding wall should be higher, with an inwards over-hanging edge, and the enclosure must embrace a pond.

Three species of terrapin are found wild in Europe. The most common is *Emys orbicularis*, popularly known as the European pond tortoise, which is found wild from north-west Africa and western Asia through southern and central Europe to Germany. (Plate C, facing p. 48.) The carapace is dark brown to black with numerous yellow spots or radiating lines on the shields. The head is brownish-black, spotted yellow. It is the largest of the European species, and reaches a length of twelve or more inches.

The other two species found in Europe are *Clemmys*

Tortoises and Terrapins

leprosa, the Spanish terrapin, found in north-west Africa and the Iberian peninsula, and the closely related *Clemmys caspica rivulata*, the Caspian terrapin, found in Yugoslavia and the Balkans and through the Greek islands and Asia Minor, to Syria. Both reach a length of about eight inches. In coloration the carapace of the Spanish is greyish to olive with a few yellowish patches on the shields; that of the Caspian is olive-green with a marbling of whitish-grey lines, with dark edges that disappear with age.

Although in the wild all three species usually hibernate in the mud at the bottom of a pond, and will do so in captivity, the unreliable British climate dictates that it is better to hibernate them indoors. They may be hibernated in a ten- to twelve-gallon aquarium, furnished with a layer of washed sand. It should be kept in an unheated room near to, but not too near, a window. Food may be offered so long as the temperature remains above fifty degrees Fahrenheit, but once the thermometer falls below it, the water should be changed (at room temperature) and the aquarium left undisturbed. In a normal winter the terrapins will remain dormant until the spring. In a mild winter the aquarium should be inspected from time to time, and if the terrapins are found to be active food should be offered to them. If taken, a day or two later the water should be changed, because urine and faeces increase the acidity of the water, which, if allowed to stagnate, will harm the eyes and damage the shells of the terrapins.

In the spring, as soon as all danger of frost is over, the terrapins may be returned to the outdoor vivarium.

If only three terrapins are found wild in Europe, by contrast America is very rich in species.

The American pond tortoise (*Emys blandingii*) is closely related to, and almost identical with, the European pond tortoise (*E. orbicularis*) mentioned on page 58. Indeed, the only difference is that the American species is the slightly larger. It is found in the area surrounding the Great Lakes and eastwards to the Atlantic coast. The painted terrapins (*Chrys-*

emys species) are so called on account of the elegantly decorated carapace. The best-known species is *C. picta* with a slightly-arched carapace that varies in colour from olive-green to brown, the marginal shields splashed with a vivid red. The southern form, *C. picta dorsalis*, may be distinguished by a light line down the centre of the carapace. They reach a length of about six or seven inches, exceptionally eight inches. Terrapins of the genus *Pseudemys* abound in the eastern states of the U.S.A. The elegant terrapin (*P. scripta elegans*) is pale brown or olive, each shield marked with black. (Plate C, facing p. 48.) It is most common in the Mississippi valley. Its eastern congener, the yellow-belly terrapin (*P. scripta scripta*) is found from North Carolina to Florida; a red-bellied, more northerly form (*P. rubriventris rubriventris*) ranges from New Jersey southward to Virginia. All three species reach a length of about nine inches. The closely-related Florida river terrapin (*P. floridana*) reaches twice this length and is, of course, a much broader and heavier animal. The carapace is olive marked with a dark, irregular pattern. The feet are fully webbed. The male has very long claws. The common map terrapin (*Graptemys geographica*) is dull olive-brown with a network of fine yellowish lines. There is a feebly-toothed keel along the carapace by which it may be distinguished from the sawback terrapin or Mississippi map terrapin (*G. pseudogeographica*) which has a pronounced dorsal keel with dark, tooth-like projections. The snapping terrapins (*Chelydra serpentina*, the common snapper, and *Macrochelys temmincki*, Temminck's or the alligator snapper) are characterized by a large head with razor-sharp jaws, a long tail and a rough or wrinkled carapace that is insufficiently large to allow complete withdrawal under it of the head, tail and legs. On account of this their only method of protection is to snap at everything in sight that moves. They make fascinating vivarium pets if it is understood that they grow to a large size and, by reason of the fact that to them attack is the only defence, must be kept by themselves. In colour they are greenish-olive to brown. The common snapper occurs from southern Canada to the Gulf of Mexico; Temminck's snapper is found mainly in the Mississippi basin.

Well-grown specimens of all these species from North America may be kept and hibernated in the same way as the European terrapins. So also may Reeve's terrapin (*Geoclemys reevesii*) from China and Japan. The carapace is dull brown sometimes mottled with grey or black. It seldom exceeds a length of six inches. A characteristic of the species is three longitudinal, dorsal keels.

Although the majority of terrapins offered for sale in this country come from Europe and the U.S.A., from time to time dealers offer some of the less hardy species that demand special care if they are not to be doomed to a premature death. They may be kept in an outdoor vivarium during the warm months, but they do not hibernate and it is, therefore, necessary to keep them fed all the year round, and never subjected to a temperature much below seventy degrees Fahrenheit. An indoor heated aqua-vivarium, necessary for their well being, must be a very large one. If this is not practical, the best solution is to transfer them to a greenhouse heated to the right temperature, and furnished with peat moss and a sunken pond of tepid water frequently changed. In such an enclosure a large number of interesting species may be kept.

The ornate terrapin, (*Pseudemys ornata*) comes from Mexico and Central America. (Plate C, facing p. 48.) Both in colour and pattern it resembles the painted terrapins of more northern latitudes, described on page 59, and to which it is very closely related.

Cope's terrapin (*Hydromedusa tectifera*) ranges from southern Brazil through Uruguay to north Argentina. It is characterized by a very long neck that can be moved very quickly when searching for food. The snout is pointed. It reaches a length of about a foot.

Very similar in appearance to the above, but rather smaller, is the long-necked terrapin (*Chelodina longicollis*) from eastern Australia, with allied species in Western Australia and Queensland. The carapace is dark brown or blackish, the legs and the upper parts of the head and neck are grey; the throat is white; the plastron yellowish. It makes an excellent pet as it spends much of its time out of water.

The helmeted terrapin (*Pelomedusa subrufa*) comes from East Africa where it is found in large numbers in the rivers and ponds. It is a rather drab species that is greyish brown all over except for the throat that is white and the plastron that is pale yellow. It reaches a length of about six or seven inches, exceptionally ten inches.

Mud terrapins are so called because they spend much time resting on, or crawling over, the mud at the bottom of a pond. In America they range from south-east Canada, through the United States and Central America, to Brazil. Those that come from the U.S.A. (*Kinosternon* species) are fairly hardy, and full-grown specimens (about four inches) will usually survive hibernation. As is only to be expected, from their way of life, they are rather drab of colour; the carapace is very dark brown to blackish, the plastron yellowish to orange-red that darkens with increasing age. Lord Derby's terrapin (*Pelusios derbianus*) and the black terrapin (*P. niger*) are two mud terrapins from Africa. Like their congeners from America both have a dark brown to black carapace—particularly the latter—and a yellowish plastron. Lord Derby's terrapin reaches a length of from fourteen to twenty inches; the black rarely exceeds six or seven inches.

Soft-shelled terrapins are so called because there are no horny plates on the skin, and the flat, circular or oval carapace is as smooth and flexible as leather. The snout ends in a short beak. There are three pointed claws on each foot and all four feet are fully webbed. The tail is short. Altogether about twenty-five different species are known and much sought after for their tasty flesh. In this country the commonest species available is *Trionyx sinensis* from China. During the summer it may be kept in an outdoor vivarium, but it must be brought indoors at nights and during the cold months; for it needs a temperature range of from sixty-eight degrees to seventy-two degrees Fahrenheit. The flat, leather-like carapace is pale brown to olive-grey in colour.

Adult terrapins are not difficult to feed. In the wild they eat mainly small fish and crustaceans, tadpoles and the like. In captivity they may be given pieces of raw meat, liver, heart, fish, water snails, earthworms, and so on. Food should be given to them in small pieces, and it is best to feed by hand to ensure that each animal gets a share and that the biggest and strongest does not scoff the lot. As they like to eat in the water, and if food is taken on land it is usually carried into the water to be eaten, until they become tame enough to take their food from between finger and thumb, the best method of feeding is to drop the food in front of them as they are swimming in the water. Food should be offered in the early evening.

At the beginning of every summer, a large number of small terrapins—each about the size of a half-crown piece—are offered for sale in the pet shops of London and the provinces. They come from North America, and most are doomed to a premature death; for few who buy them know anything of their requirements, and those from whom they buy them are not very helpful since they are concerned only with making a cash profit.

These hatchlings need special care and attention if they are to survive for more than two or three weeks, a month at most. In the first place they need a temperature of at least seventy degrees Fahrenheit to keep them feeding, and in the second place all the direct sunlight (with access to shade) that they can get.

A tank about twelve inches by eight inches by eight inches, set up as an aqua-vivarium (as described on page 18), makes a satisfactory home for two of these small terrapins. On sunny and warm days it should be placed out of doors; on cold and dull days it should be kept indoors and lighted with an electric lamp in a reflector shade about six inches above the tank, to keep the terrapins active and feeding. During the winter heat is vital; for until the terrapins reach a length of about four inches it is unwise to try and hibernate them. The water should be changed at regular intervals, to guard against pollution, and a glass cover, raised slightly at one side, should be placed over the tank if it is kept in an unheated room.

As these young terrapins are of different species and sub-species, feeding can be something of a problem because they will not all eat the same foods. Although some will accept scraped meat, shredded white fish or chopped shell fish, others will not, and will eat only live foods such as bloodworms, whiteworms (*Enchytraeus*) and very small earthworms. Still others will eat only *Daphnia* and *Tubifex*. Many need green-stuff, such as chopped lettuce, spinach, cabbage and duck-weed (*Lemna*), as part of their diet. Once they start to eat, however, they must be kept eating and every effort made to wean them to as varied a diet as possible, to include parti-cularly earthworms and scraped meat. The prepared foods sold in packets are worthless as they lack the nourishment to build their bodies and shells; so even if the terrapins eat them they more or less die of starvation.

5

Lizards and Snakes

⫸⫸

Lizards and snakes of the Class Reptilia are referred to the Order Squamata, the neuter plural of the Latin *squamatus* = scaly. They are so called because their bodies are covered with horny scales. They are adapted to life on dry land in the warmer climates. The lizards are referred to the Sub-order Sauria (Lacertilia) from the Greek *sauros* = a lizard. Apart from a few exceptions they are characterized by a very long tail, a mouth gape that is not excessively large, and although some lizards are limbless all show some trace of girdles. The snakes are referred to the Sub-order Serpentes (Ophidia), the plural of the Latin *serpens* = a serpent. The typical long slender shape is due to an elongation of the body, not to the presence of a long tail. Although some species have the rudiment of a pelvic girdle, limbs and limb girdles are absent, and movement is effected by a series of lateral waves passing backwards along the body. The tongue is sensory, and, as everyone will know, some snakes have poison fangs.

Among reptiles lizards are the most varied. They are widespread everywhere, except in the polar regions, though they occur most commonly in the tropics and become increasingly fewer as they move away from the equator. Typically the body is elongated with a long tail and two pairs of five-toed legs. When moving slowly they take long strides; at speed, however, they take short quick steps. Most are predatory, and

E
65

even those that feed on plants are not strictly vegetarian. Many do not drink water but quench their thirst by sucking the dew; those that live in deserts can tolerate a lack of moisture for long periods at a time. Most lay eggs, but in some species the egg is retained in the body of the female until it is incubated; other species are truly viviparous.

Biologically the most interesting feature of the lizard is its tail. In a few species it is short, and, like the hump of the camel, stores a reserve of food. In most, however, it is long and whip-like, and each vertebra has a central cleavage-plane at which the tail easily breaks. If the tail is seized it snaps to allow the lizard to escape. The broken tail rejuvenates in time, though seldom to the full length of the original. The phenomenon is well known to the boys of southern European countries who capture lizards with a running noose of dried grass. The method is a very ancient one, and a statue in the Vatican, from a Praxitelean original, shows that it was known to Apollo Sauroctonos, the handsome Pest Officer of antiquity. Birds are not so clever, and continue to stare in wonderment at the spasmodic contortions of the dropped tail long after the lizard has taken refuge in a crevice. Occasionally the lizard's tail is injured but unbroken and a new tail grows from the wound. It accounts for reports of lizards with two tails.

Although most lizards creep along the ground, there are some that burrow (*e.g.* the slow-worms), some that swim, and some that fly. More correctly the last are arboreal lizards which glide from branch to branch or soar against the wind with the help of a fold of skin supported by five or six elongated ribs, carried against the side of the body when not in use.

Lizards vary greatly in size: they range from the geckos, that reach no more than a few inches, to the monitors, that grow to ten or more feet. The Gila monster (*Heloderma suspectum*) found in the Gila Desert of Arizona and Mexico, and the similar, but rather larger, Mexican bearded lizard, found in western Mexico, are the only two extant species of lizard that are known to be venomous. The salivary glands of the lower jaw are con-

Lizards and Snakes

verted into poison sacs (comparable to those of venomous snakes) and the teeth form grooved fangs. To small animals the bite is quickly fatal: to man it has been known to kill and is always severe.

Only three species of lizard are found wild in the British Isles, namely the viviparous lizard, the sand lizard, and the slow-worm that is all too frequently mistaken for a snake. From time to time, either as garden escapes or by intentional introduction, colonies of the wall lizard and the green lizard are recorded as being found wild in Britain, but although they may persist for a long time in the end they die out.

The viviparous lizard (*Lacerta vivipara*) is by far the most widespread of the British species: it extends even to Ireland and is, in fact, the only reptile found wild in that country. Altogether it enjoys a very wide range, which extends from Ireland and the Bay of Biscay across the whole of central and southern Europe and central Asia to the island of Sakhalin. It is fairly resistant to cold and will tolerate neither subtropical nor tropical temperatures. It likes to be near water (into which it disappears at the approach of danger) and is equally at home in low-lying meadows and marshes and at 10,000 feet in the Alps and Caucasus. In general the colour is greyish, greenish or reddish-brown, but is very variable, and specimens that are almost black have been found. It reaches a length of from three and a half to seven inches, the tail accounting for about half. The young are born in mid-summer, so far advanced that they break open the egg case almost immediately. They are about an inch or an inch and a half long at birth and black.

The sand lizard (*Lacerta agilis agilis*) is found in central Europe from France, across Belgium, Germany and southern Sweden, to western Russia. In England it is local. A number of sub-species are found in the Balkans, and eastwards across Russia to Siberia. It favours dry and sunny districts, where it is found in rocky places, under hedges, or on heathland. The coloration varies considerably with sex, age and habitat. Males are usually greenish on the belly; females yellowish or

whitish with black spots. It reaches a length of about six to
seven and a half inches, but exceptional specimens nine and
a half inches long have been taken. The tail accounts for over
half the length.

The slow-worm (*Anguis fragilis fragilis*) is found almost
everywhere in central and western Europe (Fig. 7). In
England it is common and widespread. In southern Greece its
place is taken by *Anguis fragilis peloponnesiacus*, and east of

Fig. 7. Slow-worm (*Anguis fragilis fragilis*)

the Alps and south of the Carpathians to Iran by *Anguis
fragilis colchicus*. It has an extended snake-like body, and
externally shows no trace of legs. Despite its appearance,
however, it is a true lizard that may be distinguished from a
snake by its movable eye-lids and small shiny scales which
vary from steel-grey to coppery brown. In the wild it frequents damp woodland paths, meadows and railway embank-
ments, and hibernates either under a large stone or in a hole
in the ground. It reaches a length of about eighteen inches.

Lizards and Snakes

Clearly these three species, since they occur wild in Great Britain, may be kept in an unheated vivarium. It must be a large one, however, and for the viviparous lizard some moisture should be provided. In point of fact, they could be kept in an outdoor vivarium, only, with the exception of the slow-worm that has no legs, there is a practical difficulty in keeping in confinement lizards that are agile and can scale vertical walls.

Most of the lizards that are native to Europe may also be kept in a large vivarium at room temperature. Those most commonly imported are the wall lizard, the green lizard and the eyed lizard.

The wall lizard (*Lacerta muralis muralis*) with its many sub-species, is well-known to everyone who has visited the Continent; for it enjoys the sun and is, therefore, very common in southern Europe, where it may be seen basking on the walls of villas and churches, gardens and vineyards, and similar situations. From the Mediterranean it extends northwards through Switzerland and most of France to Belgium, Holland and western Germany. The colour varies between brown and grey. It reaches a length of about seven or eight inches.

The green lizard (*Lacerta viridis viridis*) extends across southern Europe from Portugal to the Balkans, and eastwards across Asia Minor to Iran. In coloration it varies from grass-green to yellowish green. The male is usually more yellowish than the female and has small black spots on the back; the female has large black patches. As it grows to a length of about fifteen or sixteen inches, it needs a very large vivarium.

The eyed lizard (*Lacerta lepida lepida*) also needs a very large vivarium, and one in which it can burrow, climb and move actively; for it grows to a length of about twenty inches. (Plate D, facing p. 49). It is quite an animal; in the wild, mice, other lizards and even small snakes are part of its diet, and it has been known to defend itself against dogs and cats. It can deliver a very painful bite. Though normally it lives on ground, it can, and does, spend a good deal of time climbing in low bushes. In appearance it is very similar to the green lizard, but may be distinguished by three or four rows of large blue patches, edged black, on the sides. In the wild it ranges across Spain and Portugal, and along the French and Italian rivieras and north-west Africa.

Geckos are charming little creatures that include the smallest of all reptiles. They are the only ones with a true voice; some make quite a noise for their size. They have the ability to run quickly up a perpendicular wall, and even across a ceiling. In some species, the so-called half-toed forms, the toes widen for more than half their length and are furnished with a double row of adhesive pads; in others, the so-called broad-toed forms, the toes are uniformly flat with transverse folds of skin on the undersides of the toes which serve as adhesive pads when pressed against a solid surface. In the wild, geckos are found in tropical and sub-tropical countries. As a result they need to be kept in a dry and heated vivarium. For the most part they live under stones or the bark of trees, on rocks and in the clefts of walls. Sometimes they enter houses, and are encouraged to do so as they are quite harmless and do much good in controlling flies and other insects.

The disc-fingered or Turkish gecko (*Hemidactylus turcicus turcicus*) is found in all countries that border the Mediterranean and along the coasts of the Red Sea. Eastwards it extends as far as Sind. It takes on varying shades of grey and brown, with irregular dark patches. It reaches a length of about three or four inches. It is a fussy little animal, and the loudest of the European species. When excited it carries its tail arched over its body.

The wall or Moroccan gecko (*Tarentola mauritania mauritania*) is native to the western and central countries of the Mediterranean. It is most abundant in Spain, along the Dalmatian coast and in north Africa. The colour varies from light grey to shades of yellow, brown and near-black. It moves extremely fast, and protests loudly if taken in the hand. It is rather larger than the disc-fingered gecko and averages a length of about four or five inches. Exceptionally, specimens six or seven inches long have been found. It is one of the best of the group for the vivarium, because it shows itself during the daytime, whereas most geckos are creatures of twilight.

The green gecko (*Phelsuma madagascariensis*) is another of the group that is diurnal. It comes from Madagascar, and reaches the fair size of five to six inches.

The great house gecko (*Gecko gekko*) is so named because it reaches a length of nine to eleven inches, and in south-east Asia, where it is most abundant, it is commonly seen on the walls of houses. (Plate D, facing p. 49.) The Siamese regard it as a bringer of good luck.

Chameleons are known to everyone; for, by reason of their power to change colour, they are among the show-pieces of every zoological garden. The change of colour is effected by movement of pigment granules in the pigment-cells of the skin. Their colour-changing power, however, is often exaggerated: a wide range of yellow, green and brown is possible, but they cannot come out in tartan on St. Andrew's Day. Essentially, chameleons are arboreal lizards and very highly specialized. Their toes are modified to grip branches, their tail is prehensile, and their long tongue, with a sticky tip, can be shot out at great speed to capture a fly or other suitable insect. To assist in judging distance, the eyes are large, prominent, and independently movable.

Most chameleons are native to Africa and the neighbouring island of Madagascar, but one species is to be found in India, and one, *Chamaeleo chamaeleon chamaeleon* (the common chameleon), has found its way from north Africa, Arabia, Syria and Asia Minor, into Spain and some of the islands of the Greek Archipelago. (Plate D, facing p. 49.) It reaches a length of about ten to twelve inches.

The dwarf chameleon (*Microsaura pumila*) reaches a length of only four or five inches. It is native to South Africa. It lives quite contentedly in captivity, and, if it does not change

71

colour as much as other species, has the advantage of producing its young alive. Most other species are oviparous.

For the vivarium, chameleons are not to be recommended without reservation; for they need special care if they are to survive. Warmth (a temperature range of sixty-eight degrees to seventy-seven degrees Fahrenheit) and sun are necessary, and draughts must be excluded. The vivarium must be sufficiently large for the inmates to shoot out their long tongues to catch insects, and be furnished with stout leafy branches for climbing. The leaves should be regularly sprinkled with tepid water; for in nature chameleons drink dew and though they will sometimes take maggots from a saucer they can rarely be induced to drink from one.

The iguanids are not very satisfactory for the vivarium. Most are on the large size and unattractive to the eye, like some mythological monster, with a toothed crest along the back and a throat sac that is larger or smaller. An exception may be made for the genus *Anolis*, of which some seventy species, and even more sub-species, are known.

The green or Carolina anolis (*Anolis carolinensis*) is the commonest species and the one most usually sold as a pet. It is native to the south-east of the U.S.A., Cuba and the Bahamas. Often brown by day and a shiny green at night, the male has expansible folds of skin on the throat, of a pink colour, which are spread under the influence of warmth or during courtship. It reaches a length of about six inches. In the vivarium it must be kept warm and very moist, with plenty of leafy branches for it to climb on; for like the geckos, *Anolis* species have adhesive pads on their toes that enable them to climb well. In nature they live high in trees, jump from branch to branch, or enter houses and walk over the ceilings in their search for insects to eat. Only rarely do they come to ground. Unlike geckos, however, they are diurnal.

A closely allied species is the Texas horned lizard (*Phrynosoma cornutus*) that reaches a length of only four or five inches (Fig. 8). Due to its squat appearance and a tail only about an inch long, it is more like a toad than a lizard, and, in fact, is frequently sold under the name of the horned toad. Despite its rather fearsome appearance—for short spines are distributed over its body and it has spiky horns on its head—it is quite harmless. If attacked it does not bite, but occasionally shoots drops of blood from the corners of its eyes. It is native to the U.S.A., from Kansas to Arizona, and Mexico, where it lives on the ground in dry, sandy country, into which it digs itself as soon as the day begins to cool. In captivity,

Fig. 8. Texas Horned Lizard (*Phrynosoma cornutus*)

therefore, it needs a vivarium furnished with a deep layer of dry sand, and retained at a temperature of about eighty degrees Fahrenheit. It likes to lap the moisture from sprayed leaves, but can be trained to take water from a saucer sunk in the ground.

Among lizards the skink family is the largest, with over 600 species. To the vivarium keeper it is also the least interesting, because, in nature, the majority of skinks are native to sandy-desert localities; in consequence they are somberly coloured.

F   73

Most, too, are rather lethargic—heavily-built creatures with stumpy tails. In captivity they need a heated vivarium with a deep layer of dry sand.

The sand skink (*Scincus scincus*) is native to the Sahara and the desert areas of north Africa. (Plate D, facing p. 49.) It is not an ideal animal for the vivarium; for it is very susceptible to the cold and needs a high temperature coupled with plenty of sunlight. Even at sixty-five degrees Fahrenheit it becomes motionless and quickly goes into hibernation. The body is pale yellow with brown or mauve transverse bars. It grows to a length of about eight inches.

Fig. 9. Stump-tailed Skink (*Trachydosaurus rugosus*)

A more attractive creature is the blue-tongued skink (*Tiligua scincoides*) from Australia. The name derives from the fact that the tongue, which is all the time being flicked in and out of the mouth, is of a purplish-blue colour. The body is slate-grey with dark transverse bars. It reaches a length of about nineteen inches.

Also from Australia is the stump-tailed skink (*Trachydosaurus rugosus*) so named because the tail is so short and thick that, like a modern motor car, it is hard to tell one end of the animal from the other (Fig. 9). Unlike most skinks, it has rough scales. It grows to a length of about twelve to fourteen inches, and is dark in colour with irregular yellowish spots.

Only a few skinks, of the genera *Chalcides*, *Ablephorus* and *Ophiomorus* (which is limbless), are found in Europe. The eyed skink (*Chalcides ocellatus tiliguga*) and the ocellated skink (*Chalcides ocellatus ocellatus*) are the two species most usually offered for sale in pet shops. The former reaches a length of about ten inches, the latter about six to eight inches. The colour varies greatly, but it is characteristic of the two species that the back shows a more or less regular pattern of black patches each about the same size as the scales. They inhabit the warmer districts of Greece, Crete, Sardinia and Cyprus, and extend into north Africa and across Asia Minor, Syria and Arabia to Baluchistan.

Lizards are fairly easy to feed; for the vast majority of them relish flies, moths, spiders, caterpillars, and various insects. Indeed, nowadays the most difficult part of feeding lizards is to supply them with insects that have not been in contact with toxic sprays. One solution is to breed one's own flies. Of necessity, however, it is rather unpleasant; fortunately most lizards will take gentles and mealworms which are sold as bait for coarse fishing. As an alternative, earthworms and small pieces of meat may be offered. The viviparous lizard is a ready eater of earthworms, and slow-worms like nothing better than slugs. The green lizard has been known to eat soft fruits. Chameleons need active insects, such as blue-bottles and butterflies. Mealworms are not acceptable to them, and, though they will eat most insects, they will refuse those with hard shells such as beetles. The skinks are omnivorous: they will take almost anything in the way of insects, raw meat, fruit (particularly banana), earthworms, smooth caterpillars, and even small lizards.

The feeding of snakes introduces a much more difficult problem. All snakes are carnivorous. In the wild they eat mice, rats, small birds, frogs, newts, lizards and rabbits; and the larger snakes eat even larger animals. The food is never masticated. The venomous snakes kill their prey with their poison, the non-venomous snakes by constriction, and the prey is swallowed whole. The jaw of the snake is highly specialized to allow it to open its mouth very wide; the two halves of the lower jaw separate, and so that the snake will not choke to death during the act of swallowing, the glottis is pushed out of the mouth between the separated jaw bones, whose movements are facilitated by the absence of cheekbones.

Snakes started off on the wrong foot in the Garden of Eden, and have never been able to live it down. Even if we exclude the story of Adam and Eve, of Aaron's Rod, of the Gorgons with serpents in their heads instead of hair, and other myths, the romantic novelists and *genre* artists have never allowed us to forget that it was the dreaded Egyptian cobra (*Naja haje*), as the divine minister of the Sun-god Re that deified whom it struck, which saved Cleopatra from being shamed before the Roman mob as her sister Arsinoë was shamed.

To this day, further East, its congener the Indian cobra (*Naja naja*), found from the Caspian to south China and throughout the whole of south Asia and Indonesia, is chosen by the snake charmers for their spectacular performances. Effectively deaf to all airborne sounds, the cobra does not hear the plaintive music of the gourd-pipe. When about to strike, the cobra raises about half its five-foot body into the air, spreads its spectacled hood, and sways from side to side. Good showmanship completes an act that is always less dangerous than it appears.

The peoples of the ancient world regarded the snake with a mixture of veneration and awe. We need not wonder; for there is something rather terrifying that a creature completely devoid of limbs can out-climb a monkey, out-swim a fish, and move over the ground quite unexpectedly fast. Even today, when we know how these feats are performed, most of us have an inherent aversion, a combination of fear and horror, towards snakes. Fear of their poison fangs, although only

76

about one-tenth of known species are venomous, and horror because of their gruesome method of feeding. Even the least squeamish can but be revolted at the sight of a snake constricting or poisoning a rat, a rabbit, or even a larger animal, flicking its tongue actively over it, and then engulfing it whole, the body distending as the meal passes to the stomach.

It is to be said at once, however, that in captivity it is not necessary to feed snakes with living animals, and, indeed, those who do are liable to be prosecuted by the Royal Society for the Prevention of Cruelty to Animals. In the confined space of a vivarium, an animal that is given as prey to a snake has no chance of escape and is, therefore, subject to be cruelly terrified. The Protection of Animals Act, 1911, is clear on this point and embraces all vertebrate creatures.

Those who keep snakes, therefore, must train them to take dead food. If they are not prepared to make the effort they should not keep snakes. A dead mouse, or other suitable food, warmed, because snakes are attracted to their prey by body warmth, should be held in a forceps and drawn slowly in front of the snake to simulate a living animal. If the snake does not seize the food after about five minutes it is best to leave food in the vivarium over-night, because some snakes eat only after dark.

A snake should be fed about once a week, when it should be given as much as it will eat quickly. If it does not feed at the time when food is offered to it there is no cause for alarm. A snake can go for a long time without food, and the snake probably knows best what is good for it. It may be tried with large fat earthworms or a bantam's egg; for many snakes are very partial to eggs (indeed *Dasypeltus scaber*, from Africa south of the Sahara to Sierra Leone and Abyssinia, eats little else) but forcible feeding should never be resorted to; nearly always it does more harm than good.

Although snakes are close allies of the lizards they may easily be distinguished by their long and tubular shape; it is due to an elongation of the body and not to the presence of a

77

very long tail. Limbs and (with the exception of a rudiment of a pelvic girdle in some *i.e. Python* species) limb girdles are absent. The forked tongue is sensory and harmless; the body is very distensible and in many species poison fangs are present. Always they are situated on the upper jaw, and either they have a groove running along the outer side of the tooth, or a canal running through the tooth, to convey the venom. When a bite is made the poison glands automatically pass their venom through the duct to the fangs, and into the wound.

Snakes move by a series of lateral waves passing backwards along the body. On a smooth flat surface, such as a polished dining table, a snake cannot make much progress. In the undergrowth, where it has something to push against, it can move rapidly enough; all the more so if the ground is sufficiently rough for it to gain a purchase with the scales under the body, which are attached to movable ribs and able to project and catch against any irregularities in the ground.

Snakes may be divided into two main groups; those that are venomous and those that are not. There is no certain way of distinguishing between members of each group, but to us in the British Isles it matters very little that we cannot; for no snake is found in Ireland, and of the three species found in Great Britain, only the adder or northern viper (*Vipera berus berus*) is venomous. Normally it may be distinguished by a dark zig-zag stripe along the back and an inverted V-shaped mark on the back of the head. The colour, however, is variable, and all-black specimens without the stripe sometimes occur. Any doubt that may exist about whether a snake is an adder or not may be resolved by looking at the eye, which in the adder is a vertical slit, in the other two species it is circular.

It is unwise to keep venomous snakes in a vivarium; for an escape can end in a tragedy, and however careful one is, sooner or later an escape is inevitable. We advise keeping only non-venomous snakes, and then only those that do not grow to a big size. The boa constrictor, the African python, and other members of the family Boidae are sometimes offered for sale to those with a deep purse. We advise against them too. Although they are inclined to snap only at first, and it is in their favour that they become quite docile with frequent handling, until the time that they reach seven or eight feet they do not inflict serious bites. Growth is slow, but after about five or six years they become dangerously large and usually have to be disposed of; meanwhile as they have to be kept at a temperature of seventy degrees Fahrenheit, and during the course of a year a twenty-one-foot python has been known to eat 100 chickens, four small marsupials, a kangaroo and a dog, they are expensive to keep as well as to buy in the first place:

> *A Python I should not advise—*
> *It needs a doctor for its eyes,*
> *And has the measles yearly.*

So Hilaire Belloc the wit. More appropriately, the snake that is most usually offered for sale in pet shops is the barred grass snake (*Natrix natrix helvetica*) which is found in Great Britain, decreasing in the north and absent from most of Scotland. On the Continent it ranges over western Europe from the Rhine southwards to the Pyrenees and central Italy. The general colour is greenish to brownish, with a conspicuous yellow collar, bordered posteriorily with black. When first taken it emits an evil-smelling liquid from glands near the tail, but when tame, and it soon becomes very tame, it gives up this noisome habit. In the wild it is usually found near water, and is, in fact, an excellent swimmer. Since it grows to a length of about three to four feet, and specimens from the Continent reach six feet, the vivarium should be furnished with a large water receptacle. It will feed readily on small dead frogs and toads, and may also take fish; some specimens will eat pieces of raw meat.

The smooth snake (*Coronella austriaca austriaca*) is the rarest of the British species. It is confined to the southern counties, mainly Hampshire and Dorset. On the Continent it ranges from Norway and Sweden to the north of the Iberian peninsula, and eastwards through Switzerland, central Europe and northern Greece to the Caucasus. The general colour is steel grey with parallel rows (usually four) of spots on the back. It reaches a length of about thirty inches. At first it is inclined to be vicious, but it soon becomes tame, and some specimens will even take dead mice from between finger and thumb.

These two species may be kept in an outdoor vivarium, provided it is escape-proof, but though the grass snake may be hibernated outdoors successfully under deep dry litter, it is better to hibernate the smooth snake in a frost-proof place indoors.

The species that follow come from Europe and further afield. It is better, therefore, to keep them in an indoor vivarium, which may have to be heated.

The diced, or tessellated, snake (*Natrix tessellata*) is a close relation of the grass snake (*see* p. 79) of our own countryside, and like it is usually found near water and takes the same food (Fig. 10). It ranges across Europe and Asia from the Rhineland to western China and north-west India. The general colour is greyish to olive-brown, with longitudinal rows (usually five) of square markings that are not always distinct. It reaches a length of about three to four and a half feet.

The Aesculapian snake (*Elaphe longissima longissima*) ranges across southern Europe from the Pyrenees to the Caspian and is found locally in central Europe where they are thought the descendants of specimens liberated by the Romans as sacred to the god of medicine. The general colour is yellowish-green to brown to grey, with white lines on some of the scales occasionally forming a net-work pattern. In nature it lives in open woodland, climbs well and frequently takes eggs and young birds. Mice, however, appear to be its favourite food, and in captivity most specimens will readily take them when freshly killed, also raw meat. It reaches a length of about six feet. It requires a fairly warm temperature.

The leopard snake (*Elaphe situla*) ranges across southern Europe from Malta and Sicily to the Crimea and Caucasus. (Plate D, facing p. 49.) The general colour is a light yellow or reddish grey with brownish red to orange markings edged with black. In the wild it lives in barren places, and feeds exclusively on mice and small birds. It reaches a length of about three feet.

Fig. 10. Diced Snake (*Natrix tessellata*)

The four-lined snake (*Elaphe quatuor-lineata quatuor-lineata*) reaches a length of about seven feet, and is, in fact, one of the longest of the European species. It is found in Sicily and southern Italy, through the Balkans, to Hungary and south Russia. The general colour is brown, with four black longitudinal bands. In the wild it lives in rocky places and also in woods, where it feeds on mice, moles, small birds and their eggs. It climbs well, is very strong, and makes a good pet because it rarely bites and will usually accept large earthworms.

81

Lizards and Snakes

The garter snake (*Thamnophis*) is native to America. The species usually imported for sale in pet shops is *T. sirtalis* that ranges from southern Canada to New Mexico in the east, to Minnesota in the west. The colour is very variable, but typically is a uniform brown or olive, with three yellow, red or pale green stripes. It is usually found in swampy ground, where frogs, newts and earthworms are its food. Like the grass snake (to which it is closely related) when first taken it discharges an evil-smelling liquid. It reaches a length of about three feet.

North America is rich in snakes and out of some 350 species about 300 are non-venomous. The garter snake is more or less found everywhere; for there are no less than forty-one different species of *Thamnophis*. Among the North American species the king snake (*Coronella gesula*) which is closely related to our smooth snake, and the corn snake (*Coluber guttatus*) which is closely related to the whip-snakes of Europe, are worth acquiring for their handsome appearance. The former which reaches about six feet is black with round yellow spots, or longitudinal or transverse yellow or white bands; the latter which reaches about three and a half feet is yellowish or pale brown with red, black-edged, spots along the back.

An indoor vivarium for lizards or snakes should be situated where it will catch all available sunlight, but where shade is available at the same time. It should be fairly large. For lizards the dimensions should be at least three feet by two feet by two feet, and for snakes with arboreal habits (*e.g.* the four-lined snake) it should be at least as high as the specimen is long and proportionately large, while for those snakes that spend most of their time on the ground the length of the vivarium must be the first consideration. For large snakes the vivarium should be fitted with plate glass and very strong fastenings; a snake is a powerful animal. Water for drinking should be available at all times, and a very large bowl should be provided for those species (*e.g.* the grass snake) that enjoy bathing. Rocks and large branches of trees should be included.

Lizards and Snakes

Lizards, at all events the larger ones, are extensively eaten by man. The big iguanids of tropical America and the West Indies are considered a great table delicacy, and, if we may believe E. G. Boulenger (*A Naturalist at the Dinner Table*) they are 'frequently sent by the crate-load to New York'. From very early times the Arabs have pounded the dried meat of the sand skink with date pulp, honey or oil and used it as a medicine. It is supposed an aphrodisiac and makes very good eating filleted along the backbone, soaked in beaten egg and fried in olive oil.

Snakes less rarely find their way on the menu. The African python (*Python sebae*) however, is considered a great delicacy by the natives, and Francis (Frank) Buckland, the famous Victorian naturalist, who ate most things in his time, spoke well of grilled python steak. In France the grass snake, skinned and stewed, finds its way to the table under the name of *anguille de haie* (hedge-eel). Probably it all stems from the old-time belief, perpetuated by Beaumont and Fletcher in *The Elder Brother*, that man could regain his own youth by feeding on snakes:

> *You have eat a snake*
> *And are grown young, gamesome and rampant.*

Man is omnivorous.

Crocodilians

⪼⪼⪼

A few years ago it was reported in the press that a number of alligators were thriving in the sewers under New York City. One needs to be very naïve to believe all that one reads in the newspapers, but the story has all the earmarks of truth. In time crocodilians grow to a considerable size and become dangerous, and it was brought to light that the owners, unable to find a zoo to take them over and rather than destroy them, had flushed them down the drains. Those that had survived the journey to the main sewer had made for themselves a home there, feeding on the rats.

The publicity given to the story makes it unlikely that this thoughtlessly cruel act will be repeated, but it draws attention to the fact that crocodilians are problem pets, and for this reason have been referred to an appendix, rather than given a chapter in this book. The inescapable fact is that although young crocodilians make entertaining pets, they should not be bought without first giving consideration to the future. Sooner or later they will become too big to be housed other than in a zoo, and if no zoo or other suitable organization can be found willing to take them, painless destruction remains the only solution. We do not ourselves like it.

The crocodilians (Order Crocodilia, from the Latin word *crocodilus* = a crocodile) are referred by taxonomists to three families: the gharial which contains only one species,

Appendix: Crocodilians

Gavialis gangeticus, found in the Ganges, Indus, Brahmaputra and Irrawady rivers, feeds exclusively on fish, does not attack man and is held sacred by the Indians; the true crocodiles, with about sixteen species that are represented in all the continents except Europe; and the alligators and caymans which contain seven species of which six are found in America and one, *Alligator sinensis*, in the lower reaches of the Yangtse-Kiang river of China.

Everyone will recognize a crocodilian when he sees it, though some may be hard put to distinguish between members of the three families. The gharial is characterised by a very long and narrow snout; the true crocodiles have shorter snouts than that of the gharial but that is relatively longer than those of the alligators and caymans, which are not only shorter, but broader and moderately rounded; in reality the true crocodiles are very closely related to the alligators and caymans, but may easily be distinguished by the fourth tooth of the lower jaw, which in the true crocodiles projects outside the upper jaw but in the alligators and caymans fits into a pit in the upper jaw.

For all practical purposes the only crocodilian sold in pet shops is the Mississippi alligator (*Alligator mississippiensis*). The reason is not far to seek. Its natural range is the southern states of the U.S.A. from central Texas to Florida, but it has been so persecuted for its valuable hide (and possibly out of vengeance) that it is now protected by law, and those that come to England to be sold as pets have been bred on farms and are, therefore, semi-domesticated. On land the alligator rarely attacks, and if surprised presses its body to the ground and hisses. When in the water, however, exceptionally it will attack a man, but it is not uncommon for it to pull down a dog, a sheep, or a goat, which later it will eat, but sheds no tears. Essentially aquatic, however, its main source of food, like that of all the crocodilians, is fish. In captivity, raw meat, heart, liver, and earthworms, are suitable alternatives. Food should be given daily and as much as will be eaten at a time.

Appendix: Crocodilians

On hatching the Mississippi alligator is about seven inches long, at one year about eighteen inches, at two years about two feet, at three years three feet, and at four years about four feet. Thereafter growth is slower, and it reaches its full size, of about eight to ten feet, when about fifteen years old.

A young alligator may be housed in a three-foot steel-framed glass-sided tank, filled with water to a depth of about four or five inches, and about one-third partitioned off with a sloping-sided log of wood, or smooth stones, banked up behind with washed sand, to supply a basking place. A thermo-statically-controlled electrical immersion heater should be placed in the water to keep it at between seventy-five degrees and eighty-five degrees Fahrenheit, and since a warm atmos-phere is as important as warm water the tank should be kept covered with a sheet of quarter-inch plate glass, slightly raised on thin slices of cork or wood, to allow for the free circulation of air. During the dark days of winter a sixty-watt electric lamp should be kept lighted for a few hours every day over the basking place.

The true crocodiles are not to be trusted and, therefore, they are rarely offered for sale as pets, but the caymans are, particularly the spectacled cayman (*Caiman sclerops*) from Brazil. It should be given the same treatment as the Mississippi alligator, though, as is only to be expected, it is not quite so hardy as its more northern cousin.

Provided they are given proper care and attention, crocodilians live a long time and are rarely troubled with sickness. Naturally as they grow they must be given bigger and bigger accommodation, until they become too big to be kept as pets, and, as always, cleanliness is essential: the water in the aquarium must be changed regularly with the precaution of supplying new water at the same temperature as that of the old.

Index

Index